RECIPES
1-2-3™

Also by Rozanne Gold

LITTLE MEALS:
A GREAT NEW WAY TO EAT AND COOK

Fabulous Food

Using Only Three Ingredients

Rozanne Gold

RECIPES 1-2-3™

VIKING

VIKING
Published by the Penguin Group
Penguin Books USA Inc., 375 Hudson Street,
New York, New York 10014, U.S.A.
Penguin Books Ltd, 27 Wrights Lane, London W8 5TZ, England
Penguin Books Australia Ltd, Ringwood, Victoria, Australia
Penguin Books Canada Ltd, 10 Alcorn Avenue,
Toronto, Ontario, Canada M4V 3B2
Penguin Books (N.Z.) Ltd, 182–190 Wairau Road,
Auckland 10, New Zealand

Penguin Books Ltd, Registered Offices:
Harmondsworth, Middlesex, England

First published in 1996 by Viking Penguin,
a division of Penguin Books USA Inc.

10 9 8 7 6 5 4 3 2 1

Copyright © Rozanne Gold, 1996
Photographs copyright © Tom Eckerle, 1996
All rights reserved

Recipes 1-2-3 is a trademark of Rozanne Gold.

Grateful acknowledgment is made for permission to reprint "Celery" from *Verses from 1929 On* by Ogden Nash. Copyright 1941 by Ogden Nash. First appeared in *The Saturday Evening Post*. By permission of Little, Brown and Company.

LIBRARY OF CONGRESS CATALOGING-IN-PUBLICATION DATA
Gold, Rozanne.
Recipes 1-2-3: fabulous food using only three ingredients / Rozanne Gold.
p. cm.
Includes index.
ISBN 0-670-86584-2
1. Quick and easy cookery.   I. Title.
TX833.5.G65   1996
641.5´12—dc20   95-46200

This book is printed on acid-free paper.
∞

Printed in the United States of America
Set in Minister Light
Designed by Kathryn Parise

*Just a few ingredients, of uncompromising quality,
are all you need to create exquisite recipes.*

Acknowledgments

This book is dedicated to my beautiful mother, Marion Gold, who nourishes me with her love.

Heartfelt thanks to Kim Goldstein of Canandaigua/Dunnewood Vineyards; Michele Hunter and Michael Rubin of Rubin-Hunter Communications in Santa Rosa; Lila Gault, Ann Stewart, and Marcy Posner of the William Morris Agency, who have been catalysts for great things in my life.

Special thanks to Judy Rundel and John Sheldon, my wine teachers for many years, who have shared their best vintages, their food, and friendship. Judy lent invaluable insights to the "Grapenotes."

More thanks to Chris Styler for helping to test recipes; to Helen Rothstein Kimmel, R.D., for her nutritional wizardry; and to Philip Mones, purchasing director of the Rainbow Room, for his extraordinary knowledge of ingredients.

To my editor, Dawn Drzal, may you live happily ever after;

To Fern Berman, my partner in business;

To Michael Whiteman, my partner in life.

Contents

Chapter 1

An Introduction to 1-2-3

Alimentary, My Dear: The Components of Taste

Think of the transparent sound of a small chamber orchestra; or the compressive clarity of haiku. When it comes to the senses, less is often more.

So it is with our palates and the way we taste. In addition to our keen sense of smell, the Western vocabulary contains only four descriptors for how we experience a morsel of food: salty, sour, bitter, and sweet. The Japanese posit a fifth sensation, called *umami*, a beeflike essence of wild mushrooms.

So when we confront some overwrought dishes that today's chefs bring to the table, we often are not experiencing the layers of flavor we'd like to believe, but rather a muddling or masking of basic flavor components.

A chef adds some lemon juice (an acid) to a dish, then needs to balance it with a base (perhaps cream or butter); but then it becomes bland and

needs an herb, or garlic, or sugar; and then some more acid. And so it goes. Recipes elongate into shopping lists.

This realization led me to develop *Recipes 1-2-3*™, a new repertoire of dishes based on the exquisite preparation of *three simple ingredients* of uncompromising quality—an idea so simple it took decades to come by.

Consider a slow-braising leg of lamb with forty cloves of garlic in a wine-dark broth of Côtes du Rhone: The wine reduces and permeates the meat with heady vapors, while the lamb is transformed from sinewy muscle to spoon-tender richness; the lamb's own fat becomes a kind of self-baster; and copious cloves of garlic not only perfume the meat but also thicken the sauce.

It has been said that taste is 70 percent smell; it also is true that smell stimulates appetite, and that appetite is largely anticipation. The clearly defined aromas seeping from this pot of braising lamb are therefore filling your kitchen with an irresistible kind of culinary foreplay.

Yes, only three ingredients. No, this is not "Minimalist" cuisine.

Taste, a complex realm that transcends the mere ingredients of a dish, plays upon our memories, our cultures, and quite probably on our genes. It takes only a few components of a recipe to trigger a cavalcade of flavors, sensations, and long-lost recollections—and once that is accomplished we should learn that enough is truly enough, that what we've cooked has fulfilled our nutritional and emotional objectives.

In my twenty years as a professional chef, I've imposed dozens of ingredients onto a single dish; used paintbrushes and squeeze bottles to decorate plates; piled food so precariously as to challenge gravity.

Turnabout: Today I'm convinced that we really can create delicious food and orchestrate wonderful meals by combining recipes with just a few ingredients. Perfect for today's cook, these formulations result in dishes that are concentrated in flavor and elemental in taste.

Of course there are other sensory aspects to eating, among them sight, sound, and touch. Surely we feast with our eyes and revel in the sound of clinking glasses. Food always touches our lips, our tongues, and the insides of our mouths, letting us experience the variance of texture and temperature.

And, always, good food touches our hearts.

A Personal Guarantee

I promise you will never think about cooking in the same way again. For me, 1-2-3 has become an intellectual gambol, as well as a satisfying effort to preserve the pleasures of the table.

When I get an idea for a recipe—or see a dish on a menu, or beautiful food in a magazine—I immediately ask myself: What are the elemental flavors? How can I achieve them simply?

Do not misconstrue: The title, *Recipes 1-2-3*, of this book is not synonymous with fast food, nor exclusively with quick-and-easy. This is not an I-hate-to-cook book.

Recipes using only three ingredients are extraordinarily liberating: The cook can kiss the drudgery of shopping good-bye, and the meal, freed from "ingredient-overload," can now be true to itself. There are always tradeoffs, however.

For example, you may reinvest *some* of that saved shopping time in meticulous attention to dicing, mincing, and julienning—because certain dishes require ingredients of specific size and shape to help define flavor.

Other recipes gain their character by gentle coaxing: slow cooking, oven-roasting, braising, caramelizing—all requiring time to undergo a supernal transformation. This doesn't mean you're implacably tied to the kitchen, for you can weed the garden, hug your spouse, or dress for dinner while low heat performs its inevitable magic.

To be sure, many recipes in this book *are* 1-2-3 in terms of both time *and* ingredients. They are "sciue-sciue," or quick-quick in Italian, requiring a flash in the pan, a quick steam bath, or seconds in a blender.

Still other recipes focus on simple but artful presentation: a juicy summer tomato, milky-sweet fresh mozzarella, and fragrant basil are so taken for granted that they need to be presented in dramatic ways to make them seem new again.

And there's a bonus: By limiting recipes to three components and by aiming for intense flavor, I've been forced to eliminate extra fat—sometimes *any* fat—which means many of these dishes are surprisingly low in calories.

With the hassles of shopping and the manipulation of many ingredients dramatically minimized, my personal guarantee is that *Recipes 1-2-3* will get you *cooking* again.

Chapter 2

Recipes 1-2-3:
Course by Course

*A*n important goal of this book is to make cooking more user-friendly—without taking any shortcuts.

A second goal is to sweep away the excesses of overly complicated recipes—and thereby to explore a new directness and clarity of flavor that comes from simplicity.

Another goal is to establish more intimate acquaintance with each ingredient—to demonstrate how a roasted asparagus stalk differs from one that's steamed; why baked squash makes a different (and better) soup than one that's boiled; how you can cook a voluptuous stew without browning meat in puddles of fat; how you can use one ingredient in several different ways.

A final goal: To prove that you can prepare a three-course dinner for six and still make it through the express lane at your supermarket!

Party Food and Appetizers

Little Cod Beignets
Cherry Tomato Bonbons
Eggplant on Fire
La Mort du Camembert
Lemony Tahina
Black Hummus
Sherry Vinegar Mushrooms
Extra-Bonus Mushroom Pâté
Cornmeal-Pasta Chips
Tiny Pepper Cheese Crackers
Party Wraps:
　　Grape Leaves and Haloumi
　　Radicchio and Smoked Mozzarella
　　Pancetta and Boccancini
Lacquered Chicken Wings
Med-Rim Lamb Nuggets, I and II
Angels and Archangels on Horseback
Fried Chickpeas with Sage and Walnut Oil
Rosettes of Smoked Salmon on Cucumber Rounds
Parmesan Lace Galettes
Ouzo Feta Spread
Wine-Baked Olives
Venetian Wafers
Brillat-Savarin's Fondue
Flying Saucers

Arugula and Mussel Salad, Anchovy Vinaigrette
Farmhouse Cheddar Frittata
Iceberg Hearts, Bacon, and Blue Cheese Dressing
Swedish Cured Salmon
Bresaola and Asiago "Carpaccio," Truffle Oil
Celery Rémoulade, Celeriac Chips
Roasted Red Peppers, Yellow Pepper Puree
Veal Sausage with Asparagus Sauce and Asparagus Tips
Pan-Roast Oysters with Butter and Leeks
Checkerboard Orzo Salad
Niçoise Socca Crêpe, Marinated Goat Cheese
Asparagus and Prosciutto Bundles, Melted Fontina
Mesclun and Blood Orange Salad, Orange Vinaigrette
Grilled Shiitake Mushrooms, Garlic Essence
Seared Sea Scallops on Sweet Pea Puree
Smoked Salmon "Pitza"
Tomato, Mozzarella, and Basil: Six Styles
Salad Frisée with Lardons and Hot Vinegar Dressing

First Courses

Salmon Carpaccio Cooked on a Plate
Salad of Roasted Beets and Beet Greens, Walnut Oil
Shrimp with a Kiss

Soups and Pasta

Carrot-Ginger Velvet
Port Consommé
"Cream" of Spinach Soup
Fournade: Creamy Chickpea Soup

Soupy Red Beans with Smoked Ham
Avocado Velouté, Fino Sherry
Fennel, Leek, and Orzo Soup
Curried Lentil Soup
"Fire and Ice" Gazpacho
Chicken Broth 1-2-3
"Sopa de Salsa"
Yellow Turnip Soubise
Beer and Stilton Soup
Red Wine Onion Soup
An Unusual Borscht: Roasted Beet,
    Squash, and Yogurt
Chilled Cauliflower Crème
Brie and Pear Soup
Ginger Pepperpot, "Glass" Noodles
Sauerkraut "Hangover" Soup
Yellow Pea and Bacon Potage
Veal Tortellini, Turkish Yogurt Sauce
Garlic and Oil Spaghetti
Linguine Riviera, Red Sardine Sauce
Cheese Raviolini, Roasted Pumpkin
    Sauce
Hungarian Cabbage and Noodles
Farfalle with Broccoli, Broccoli-Butter
    Sauce
Orecchiette with Endive and Sun-Dried
    Tomatoes
Angel's Food:
    Angel Hair Pasta with Caviar
    Angel Hair Pasta with Truffle Oil
A Very Old Neapolitan Pasta: Macaroni
    and Tomatoes
Spinach Fettuccine with Tomato Butter
Penne and Pencil Asparagus, Torta di
    Mascarpone

MAIN COURSES

Steamed Clams in Thyme Butter
Barbecue Pepper Shrimp
Tuna Burgers, Hoisin, and Pickled
    Ginger
Red Snapper in Burnt Orange Oil
Crispy Salmon with Pancetta and Sage
Roast Cod with Red Pepper Puree
Rosemary-Infused Swordfish
Pepper-Seared Tuna, Cool Mango Relish
Steamed Halibut, Bell Pepper Confetti
Salmon Baked in Grape Leaves
Pan-Seared Tuna Niçoise, Tomato
    "Water"
Two-Way Salmon and Zucchini:
    Poached Salmon with Zucchini, Two
        Sauces
    Pan-Seared Salmon, Creamy Zucchini
        Sauce
Perfect Chicken Salad
Chicken Roasted in a Salt Crust
Poulet Rôti with Wild Mushrooms
Country-Fried Chicken
Chicken-in-a-Watermelon
Chicken "Villagio," Diced Lemon Sauce
Yogurt Chicken with Blackened Onions
Cornish Hen Under a Brick
Brine-Cured Cornish Hens, Glazed
    Shallots and Parsnip Puree
One Duck, Two Dinners:
    Braised Duck Legs with Apples and
        Sauerkraut
    Sautéed Duck Breasts with Green
        Olives and Sweet Vermouth

Michael's Perfect Roast Turkey with
  Lemon and Sage
Veal Roast with Leeks and Rosé Wine
Osso Buco with Tomatoes and Black
  Olives
Grilled Veal Chop, Yellow Tomato Coulis,
  and Basil Oil
Arista: Roast Pork Loin with Rosemary
  and Garlic
Barbecued Pork Pull
Pork Chops with Vinegar Peppers
Roast Pork Tenderloin with Prunes and
  Bay Leaves
Garlic Sausage, Lentils, and Diced
  Carrots
Calf's Liver with Home-Dried Grapes
Lamb Shanks Alsatian-Style
Lamb Steaks with Tomatoes and Za'atar
Rack of Lamb with Pesto Crumbs
Turkish Lamb Chops
Maple-Glazed Corned Beef
Coffee and Vinegar Pot Roast
Steak Haché, Cabernet Butter
Pan-Seared Sirloin, Oyster Sauce
  Reduction
Mahogany Short Ribs
Fillet of Beef, Gorgonzola Whipped
  Potatoes
Prime Ribs of Beef, Horseradish-Rye
  Crust

VEGETABLES AND SIDE DISHES

Caramelized Endive and Bacon
Turnip and Havarti Torte
Fried Lemon and Zucchini Salad
Hubbard Squash and Orange Puree
Turkish Pilaf with Tomato
Watercress Puree
French Beans with Toasted Hazelnuts
Zucchini, Black Olive, and Tomato
  Compote
Whole Roasted Garlic with Goat Cheese
Rosemary-Roasted Potatoes
Smothered Lettuce with Sumac
Steamed Broccoli, Stir-Fried Pecans
Spoonbread Custard
White Polenta with Parmigiano-Reggiano
Potato-Fennel Mash
Sugar Snaps in Orange Butter
Gratin Dauphinoise
Dry-Curry Sweet Potatoes
Barley-Buttermilk Salad
Bay-Smoked Potatoes
Broccoli di Rape I-II-III
Chardonnay Cabbage
Two-Way Grits:
  Cheddar-Pepper
  Garlic
Yucca "Hash Browns" with Red Pepper
Creamed Potatoes, Swedish-Style
Wilted Cucumbers, Dill Butter
Wild Rice and Bulghur Toss
Braised Celery Batons, Fried Celery
  Leaves
Baked Sweet Fennel, Parmesan Crust

Pan-Grilled Radicchio, Fried Rosemary
French Potato Cake
Giant Glazed Onions, Balsamic Vinegar
Crisp Eggplant Tassels
Oven-Roasted Asparagus, Fried Capers
Saffron Orzo
Cumin-Scented Couscous
Aromatic Ginger Rice
Egg Noodles with Butter and Rosemary
Orange and Gold Potato Puree, Sweet
    Potato Chips
Husk-Roasted Corn, Chili Butter
Perfect Mashed Potatoes
Tender White Beans with Tarragon
Ultra Tomatoes:
    Slow-Roasted Romas
    Melted Tomatoes

DESSERTS AND OTHER SWEET THINGS

Green Apple and Lychee Tart
Frozen Maple Soufflé
Dark Chocolate Mousse
Alice B. Toklas's Sugar Candy
Lemon Buttermilk Ice Cream
Strawberries in Grappa
Corsetière's Despair
Pastel Easter Sorbet
Chocolate Bread Pudding
Iced Maple Custard, Warm Maple Syrup
Black Walnut Bars
Chocolate Banana Terrine
Prune Jelly with Prune Pips
Fresh Blueberries, Lemon Curd Cream

Chocolate Milk Pudding
Chianti Granita
Raspberry Cloud Soufflé
Green Melon Zabaglione
Maple Mousse Parfait
Syrian Shortbread
Bittersweet Cocoa Sorbet
Eggnog and Panettone Bread Pudding
Oven-Roasted Strawberries, Fresh Straw-
    berry Sorbet
"Love of Three Oranges":
    Orange Ambrosia
    Marsala Oranges with Toasted Pignoli
    Orange, Walnut, and Pomegranate
      Salad
Cold Rhubarb Soup, Mascarpone
    "Quenelle"
Vanilla Sugar Cigars
Pepper Lime Ice Cream
Fresh Berry "Kir Imperial"
Little Lemons Filled with Lemon Yogurt
    "Gelato"
Chocolate Truffle Torte
"Cannoli" Custard
Strawberry Summer Pudding
Caramelized Pineapple, Black Pepper
    Syrup
Poires Belle-Hélène, Pear Sorbet
Pumpkin Pavé
Yogurt "Coeur à la Crème," Apricot
    Compote
Napoleon of Roquefort and Sauternes
Snitz Pie
Almond Brittle from Sicily
Mixed Fruit Rumtopf

GRACE NOTES

Chapter 3

About the Recipes

Ingredients

Every recipe in this book is based on just three carefully balanced ingredients. Water, salt, and pepper—fundamental to all cooking—are "free."

- *Water* means tap water, or bottled or filtered water if your environment requires it.
- *Salt* can mean iodized table salt; kosher salt; sea salt, coarse and fine; and geographically specific salts, such as French and Italian.
- *Pepper* can mean white or black peppercorns, whole or freshly ground in a mill; and coarse butcher-grind or mignonette black pepper, which you can find prepackaged.

Each recipe specifies which types of salt and pepper to use, and when. Because my recipes are *about* their ingredients, nothing can mask inferior

quality. So you must be willing to trade up a bit, or journey to a specialty-food shop for the very best of what is required.

Few supermarket cheeses come close to the singular taste of Parmigiano Reggiano grated by hand as needed; cheap acidic vinegar will ruin a dish that calls for wonderfully mellowed wine vinegar; you dare not substitute margarine for butter or corn oil for honest olive oil without upsetting the balance of a dish—indeed, you may destroy its very validity.

Although we pretend to escape dependency on the seasonal cycles of nature, we delude ourselves. Raspberries shipped from Chile in sealed gas containers in December, broccoli harvested before a frost, tomatoes plucked green and trucked two thousand miles—all are dilute imitations of the real thing that seduce our appetites but corrupt our tastes.

So this book contains a "Calendar of Menus," organized to make the most of products at their seasonal peaks—when, coincidentally, they are cheapest and most flavorful.

In addition, *Recipes 1-2-3* includes serving suggestions, presentation tips, and "add-ons," for free kitchen spirits who want to add a bit more complexity to dishes—and have time to do it.

The 1-2-3 Pantry

"Convenience food" has a pejorative ring; some might call it "shelf indulgence," but my kitchen cabinet is filled with convenience foods!

Thanks to first-rate ingredients, gleaned from around the world, my cupboard brims with maroon sun-dried tomatoes; premium olive oils from Spain, Italy, California, and Israel; jars of coal-black olive puree; Chinese oyster sauce and hoisin sauce; piquant and exotic pomegranate molasses; anchovies and capers coiled in oil, spicy harissa in collapsible tubes, and za'atar—a Middle Eastern spice blend of hyssop, sumac, and sesame seeds.

Convenient? You bet.

I mix granulated sugar with cinnamon, and some with vanilla beans, to have quick dessert flavorings right at hand.

My freezer is home to sheets of puff pastry, phyllo dough, pesto, and pita bread—in case I don't have the time to make my own.

Although we all agree that a long-simmering homemade stock is preferable, some canned products are nonetheless acceptable. I strongly suggest a supply of Chicken Broth 1-2-3 in your freezer, however (page 96).

Late-summer tomatoes make voluptuous sauce, but what about the rest of the year? Pomi brand strained tomatoes and canned Italian plum tomatoes in puree become a better option.

Best of all, many of our new conveniences are of a very high order—flavored oils (either homemade or store-bought), roasted garlic puree, provocative vinegars such as my Herbes de Provence Vinegar (page 69), exotic styles of mustard, pickles, chutneys, and chowchows—and they facilitate the task of making intensely flavored dishes that are vivid, rich, and bold.

For the modern cook these ideologically acceptable conveniences induce what I call ISR, or "instant salivary response."

A Note on Salt

All salt is not created equal. Various salts taste different from one another and affect foods accordingly. Common salt has additives (generally dextrose, and tricalcium phosphate to keep granules from sticking); iodized salt has sodium iodide added. Kosher salt, with its coarser flakes, gives food a brighter taste and is unadulterated. Coarser still are sea salts, evaporated from seawater and retaining trace minerals, which in addition to perking up foods impart an appealing crunch when used at the very last minute.

I like French sea salt, and am thrilled when my friend Francesco de'Rogati brings a box of Italian sea salt from his yearly sojourns. French (*gros sel*) and Italian (*sale marino grosso*) sea salts can be used interchangeably.

For *Recipes 1-2-3* use table salt, iodized or not, when the recipe denotes "salt." Use kosher salt when the recipe calls for "coarse salt." Use sea salt, from anywhere, when it is specified.

It's also fun to experiment with other salts—like Hawaiian alae salt, which is coarse sea salt reddened by Hawaiian clay.

A Note on Pepper

In America, pepper mills are filled with whole black peppercorns. In France, they are filled with white.

At home I use both and have two pepper mills near my stove: a large one with black peppercorns and the smaller filled with white. I prefer the assertive taste and pungency of the black peppercorn and use it more often.

White peppercorns have a wonderful camphor-like essence and a unique taste perfect for seasoning specific foods. White pepper is also preferred for cream or butter sauces, or sauces light in color or texture.

Specific varieties of black pepper are interesting to use. Tellicherry, for example, has spicy sweet heat and a hint of pine.

Both black and white peppercorns are the small dried fruit of an East Indian plant. Black peppercorns are the unripe, sun-dried whole berry. White peppercorns are allowed to ripen completely and are the internal part of the berry.

My 1-2-3 Pantry Staples

Quick and easy recipes that should always be available and ready to use:

Basil Oil	p. 156
Garlic Oil	p. 52
Herbes de Provence Vinegar	p. 69
Labaneh (Yogurt Cheese)	p. 111
Black Olive Tapenade	p. 36
Vanilla Sugar	p. 224
Cinnamon Sugar	p. 224

Chapter 4

Food and Wine Together

"This wine should be eaten, it is too good to be drunk."

—Jonathan Swift

any of the recipes in this book are for simple foods with complex flavors. I've made a variety of recommendations for food and wine pairings, called "Grapenotes," but the most fun of all is making your own discoveries.

As Culinary Counselor for Dunnewood Vineyards, I have spent the last few years conducting food-and-wine seminars for distributors, chefs and restaurateurs, consumers, and food and wine writers all over the country. It's wonderful to explore the components of taste with unsuspecting subjects who little imagine they will never again taste food and wine together in quite the same way.

Not only do we break every rule in the book—finding wines that taste great with artichokes, preferring a cabernet over a chardonnay with

"Seared Salmon on a Moroccan Salad," or discovering how a drizzle of honey on feta cheese will redirect the palate to a particular wine—but we learn several palate-liberating principles:

1. No two people perceive food or wine in the identical manner.
2. The *preparation* of a dish is what matters most in matching food with wine.
3. Equally important as matching flavors is matching the weight or body of a particular dish with the body of a particular wine.
4. Our responses to the effects of food with wine are clearly physiological and emotional.
5. The sense of smell is a major player in food and wine pairing. Next comes taste—and all sensory systems connected to it.
6. There may be several different wines, of various colors and characteristics, that will go beautifully with the *same* dish.
7. The marriage of food and wine also speaks to the seasons. While duck braised with turnips and mushrooms is a weighty dish, calling for wines of substance, a spicy chilled Gewürztraminer can make it taste like summer, while a warm Rhône red is more appropriate on blustery days.
8. Your own palate is the only important frame of reference for what works—

and what doesn't. Finding out why is a lifelong dialogue with your senses.

I love to ask friends, professional and otherwise, about food and wine combinations that dispel preconceived ideas. My husband enjoys country pâté with an off-dry sauvignon blanc; food critic Arthur Schwartz is crazy about salty taramasalata and sweet German Spatlese; British wine expert Jancis Robinson likes to drink a big white French Burgundy with venison; wine guru Kevin Zraly craves a lighter-style crianza Rioja (red) with Dover sole; wine writer Dan Berger likes smoked mozzarella and tomato salad with ten-year-old Carneros pinot noir. Others believe that cabernet sauvignon goes with chocolate cake, and I love gamay beaujolais with dense, creamy cheesecake.

Because so many new *types* of wines are flooding the marketplace, it's time to rewrite the old rules anyway. Italians make chardonnay and cabernet sauvignon that taste quite different from what comes from California or France. The French are "deconstructing" their blended wines into separate components, so today you can buy their marsanne, cabernet franc, ugni blanc, or mourvedre.

For good measure, we're growing sangiovese and nebbiolo in California, as well as viognier, syrah, and charbono—and conventional wisdom says nothing about how these Old World wines with New

World tastes are supposed to link with food.

What goes well with a smoked duck burrito, or Thai-style shrimp with galangal and lemongrass, anyway?

If the world is your wine list, then you are your own Christopher Columbus on an uncharted wine-dark sea.

Chapter 5

A Calendar of Menus

"If you can capture the season on a plate, then you are the master."
—Japanese proverb

*A*ppetite, properly seduced, has a hard time saying no.

A beautifully orchestrated menu, in harmony with the seasons, is the first step in alerting the senses. For the language of menus is meant to make us hunger.

Playful, enticing-sounding menus can evoke vivid taste memories or trigger sensory responses even before we touch a morsel of food. Each course of a well-balanced menu gently moves the appetite along—from anticipation to satisfaction.

Recipes 1-2-3 features fifty-two menus, one for every week of the year, coordinated with the seasons and linked with time-honored holidays and celebrations.

In many cases, entire three-course dinner parties can be assembled using only nine to twelve ingredients.

JANUARY

New Year's Day Brunch Buffet
Sauerkraut "Hangover" Soup
Swedish Cured Salmon
Creamed Potatoes, Swedish-Style
Flying Saucers
Brillat-Savarin's Fondue
Caramelized Endive and Bacon
Grapefruit in Campari Syrup,
Crystallized Grapefruit

Italian Family Dinner
Fennel, Leek, and Orzo Soup
Chicken "Villagio," Diced Lemon Sauce
White Polenta with Parmigiano-Reggiano
Marsala Oranges with Toasted Pignoli

Dinner Party
Salmon Carpaccio Cooked on a Plate
Rack of Lamb with Pesto Crumbs
Tender White Beans with Tarragon
Baked Sweet Fennel, Parmesan Crust
Chocolate Bread Pudding

Saturday Lunch
Salad Frisée with Lardons and Hot
Vinegar Dressing
Farmhouse Cheddar Frittata
Yucca "Hash Browns" with Red Pepper
Black Walnut Bars

Sunday Supper
Yellow Pea and Bacon Potage
Fillet of Beef, Gorgonzola
Whipped Potatoes
French Beans with Toasted Hazelnuts
Chutney Baked Apples, Vanilla Cream

FEBRUARY

Family Dinner
Iceberg Hearts, Bacon, and Blue
Cheese Dressing
Chicken Roasted in a Salt Crust,
Braised Celery Batons, Fried
Celery Leaves
Snitz Pie

Valentine's Day Dinner
Angels and Archangels on Horseback
Shrimp with a Kiss
Braised Veal Roast with Leeks
and Rosé Wine
Perfect Mashed Potatoes
Raspberry Cloud Soufflé

Sunday Brunch
Celery Rémoulade, Celeriac Chips
Roast Cod with Red Pepper Puree
Spoonbread Custard
Sliced Lemon Pie

Dinner Party
Bresaola and Asiago "Carpaccio,"
Truffle Oil

Crispy Salmon with Pancetta and Sage
Potato-Fennel Mash
Slow-Roasted Romas
Bittersweet Cocoa Sorbet
Almond Brittle from Sicily

MARCH

St. Patrick's Day
Beer and Stilton Soup
Maple-Glazed Corned Beef
Chardonnay Cabbage
Beer Bread
Green Melon Zabaglione

A Med-Rim Dinner Party
Fournade: Creamy Chickpea Soup
Turkish Lamb Chops or Salmon Baked in
Grape Leaves
Turkish Pilaf with Tomato
Fried Lemon and Zucchini Salad
Yogurt Coeur à la Crème, Apricot
Compote

An Afternoon Tea
Avocado Velouté, Fino Sherry
Napoleon of Roquefort and Sauternes
Mesclun and Blood Orange Salad,
Orange Vinaigrette
Alice B. Toklas's Sugar Candy

Breakfast in Bed
Orange Ambrosia
Spoonbread *Pain Perdu* with Strawberry
Spoon Fruit

Frozen Hot Chocolate
Cinnamon Croûtes

Family Dinner
Hungarian Cabbage and Noodles
Roast Pork Tenderloin with Prunes and
Bay Leaves
Hubbard Squash and Orange Puree
Frozen Maple Soufflé

APRIL

April Fools' Day
Cherry Tomato Bonbons
La Mort du Camembert
Chicken-in-a-Watermelon
Garlic Grits
Prune Jelly with Prune Pips

Passover Dinner
Salad of Roasted Beets and Beet Greens,
Walnut Oil
"Brine-Cured" Cornish Hens, Glazed
Shallots and Parsnip Puree
Caramelized Pineapple,
Black Pepper Syrup

A Vegetarian Lunch
Roasted Red Peppers, Yellow
Pepper Puree
Checkerboard Orzo Salad
Grilled Shiitake Mushrooms,
Garlic Essence
Lemon Buttermilk Ice Cream

April in Paris:
Supper at the Wine Bar
Red Wine Onion Soup
Calf's Liver with Home-Dried Grapes
Gratin Dauphinoise
Pots de Crème: Chocolat

Easter Sunday
Niçoise Socca Crêpe, Marinated
Goat Cheese
Lamb Shanks Alsatian-Style
Melted Tomatoes
Oven-Roasted Asparagus, Fried Capers
Pastel Easter Sorbet

MAY

A May Day Dinner
Asparagus and Prosciutto Bundles,
Melted Fontina
Rosemary-Infused Swordfish
Zucchini, Black Olive, and
Tomato Compote
Cumin-Scented Couscous
Cold Rhubarb Soup, Mascarpone
"Quenelle"

Mother's Day Celebration
Brie and Pear Soup
Poached Salmon with Zucchini,
Two Sauces
Watercress Puree and Creamed Potatoes
Oven-Roasted Strawberries, Fresh
Strawberry Sorbet

Dinner from a French Café
Veal Sausage with Asparagus Sauce and
Asparagus Tips
Poulet Rôti with Wild Mushrooms
Egg Noodles with Butter and Rosemary
Dark Chocolate Mousse

Sunday Supper
"Cream" of Spinach Soup
Tiny Pepper Cheese Crackers
Yogurt Chicken with Blackened Onions
Barley-Buttermilk Salad
Turkish Cherry Bread

JUNE
A Weekday Dinner
Spinach Fettuccine with Tomato Butter
Pork Chops with Vinegar Peppers
Rosemary-Roasted Potatoes
"Cannoli" Custard

Father's Day
Barbecue Pepper Shrimp
Pan-Seared Sirloin, Oyster Sauce
Reduction
French Potato Cake
Chocolate Banana Terrine

Saturday Lunch on the Porch
Soupy Red Beans with Smoked Ham
Country-Fried Chicken
Celery Rémoulade, Celeriac Chips
Fresh Blueberries, Lemon Curd Cream
Twice-Baked Oatcakes

Summer Dinner Party
Penne and Pencil Asparagus, Torta di
Mascarpone
Pan-Seared Tuna Niçoise,
Tomato "Water"
Parmesan Lace Galettes
Fresh Berry "Kir Imperial"
Vanilla Sugar "Cigars"

JULY

July 4th Fireworks
Little Cod Beignets
"Fire and Ice" Gazpacho
Pan-Seared Salmon, Creamy
Zucchini Sauce
Husk-Roasted Corn, Chili Butter
Pepper Lime Ice Cream

Dinner, Trattoria-Style
Crisp Eggplant Tassels
Osso Buco with Tomatoes and
Black Olives
Saffron Orzo
Chianti Granita

Summer Bistro Supper
Seared Sea Scallops on Sweet Pea Puree
Sautéed Duck Breasts with Green Olives
and Sweet Vermouth
Pan-Grilled Radicchio, Fried Rosemary
Pots de Crème: Vanille

A Mezze Sampler
Eggplant on Fire
Lemony Tahina

Ouzo Feta Spread
Black Hummus
Grape Leaves and Haloumi
Za'atar Pita
Med-Rim Lamb Nuggets, I and II
Syrian Shortbread
Iced Bedouin Coffee

AUGUST

Summer Picnic
Tomato, Mozzarella, and Basil "Club"
Wine-Baked Olives
Perfect Chicken Salad
Baked Sweet Fennel, Parmesan Crust
Granola Fruit Cobbler

A Special Luncheon
An Unusual Borscht: Roasted Beet,
Squash, and Yogurt
Red Snapper in Burnt Orange Oil
Aromatic Ginger Rice
Wilted Cucumbers, Dill Butter
Fresh Strawberry Sorbet
Sweet Zwieback

A Summer Supper
Arugula and Mussel Salad,
Anchovy Vinaigrette
Orecchiette with Endive and Sun-
Dried Tomatoes
Amaretto "Creamsicle" in Frozen
Oranges

Family Celebration
Farfalle with Broccoli, Broccoli-
Butter Sauce
Steamed Halibut, Bell Pepper Confetti
Braised Celery Batons, Fried
Celery Leaves
Strawberry Summer Pudding

Tex-Mex Fest
"Sopa de Salsa"
Crisp Tortilla Ribbons
Pepper-Seared Tuna, Cool Mango Relish
Red Onion Salad
Bittersweet Cocoa Sorbet, Cinnamon-
Sugar Cigars

SEPTEMBER

Labor Day Bash
Steamed Clams in Thyme Butter
Barbecued Pork Pull
Cheddar-Pepper Grits
Giant Glazed Onions, Balsamic Vinegar
Corsetière's Despair

Italian Farmhouse Dinner
Cheese Raviolini, Roasted
Pumpkin Sauce
Arista: Roast Pork Loin with Rosemary
and Garlic
Broccoli di Rape with Anchovy and
Toasted Pignoli
Fresh pears, grapes, and Pecorino cheese

Candlelight Supper
Curried Lentil Soup
Grilled Veal Chop, Yellow Tomato Coulis,
and Basil Oil
Slow-Roasted Romas
Perfect Mashed Potatoes
Maple Mousse Parfait

Dining-Light Dinner
Sherry Vinegar Mushrooms
Mushroom Pâté Crostini
Linguine Riviera, Red Sardine Sauce
Little Lemons Filled with Lemon
Yogurt "Gelato"

OCTOBER

Autumn Dinner Party
Veal Tortellini, Turkish Yogurt Sauce
Lamb Steaks with Tomatoes and Za'atar
Smothered Lettuce with Sumac
Black Hummus, served warm
Poires Belle-Hélène, Pear Sorbet

"La Spaghetatta"
Antipasti: Cornmeal-Pasta Chips
Venetian Wafers
Fried Chickpeas with Sage and
Walnut Oil
Radicchio and Smoked Mozzarella
Pancetta and Boccancini
Garlic and Oil Spaghetti
Broccoli di Rape with Garlic and Oil
A platter of ripe fresh figs

Halloween Supper
Carrot-Ginger Velvet
Mahogany Short Ribs
Orange and Gold Potato Puree, Sweet
Potato Chips
Chocolate Milk Pudding
Candy corn

Far East Flavors
Lacquered Chicken Wings
Ginger Pepperpot, "Glass" Noodles
Tuna Burgers, Hoisin, and Pickled
Ginger
Steamed Broccoli, Stir-Fried Pecans
Green Apple and Lychee Tart

NOVEMBER

Italian Regional Dinner
A Very Old Neapolitan Recipe: Macaroni
and Tomatoes
Cornish Hen Under a Brick
Bay-Smoked Potatoes
Broccoli di Rape with White Raisins
Strawberries in Grappa

Thanksgiving Dinner
Yellow Turnip Soubise
Michael's Perfect Roast Turkey with
Lemon and Sage
Wild Rice and Bulghur Toss
Dry-Curry Sweet Potatoes
Cranberry Chutney
Pumpkin Pavé

Warming Winter Lunch
Steak Haché, Cabernet Butter
Gratin Dauphinoise
Whole Roasted Garlic with Goat Cheese
Iced Maple Custard, Warm Maple Syrup

Supper in Your Silk Pajamas
Smoked Salmon "Pitza"
Angel's Food: Angel Hair Pasta with
Caviar or Truffle Oil
Strawberries and Candied Ginger
Dipped in Chocolate

DECEMBER

Hanukkah Celebration
Chicken Broth 1-2-3
Coffee and Vinegar Pot Roast
French Potato Cake
Red Wine Apple Sauce
Hazelnut Tea Cake

The Night Before Christmas
Port Consommé
Braised Duck Legs with Apples
and Sauerkraut
Orange, Walnut, and Pomegranate Salad
Eggnog and Panettone Bread Pudding

Grand Holiday Dinner

Pan-Roast Oysters with Butter
and Leeks
Prime Ribs of Beef, Horseradish-
Rye Crust
Turnip and Havarti Torte
Sugar Snaps in Orange Butter
Chocolate Truffle Torte

New Year's Eve Open House

Rosettes of Smoked Salmon on
Cucumber Rounds
Chilled Cauliflower Crème, Black Caviar
Garlic Sausage, Lentils, and
Diced Carrots
Mixed Fruit Rumtopf Flambé
Sweet Zwieback

Chapter 6

Party Food and Appetizers

*P*arty food is snap, crackle, and pop for adults.

Small and savory, these little morsels resonate with piquancy. They nuzzle our palates. They excite a desire for more. They make us thirst.

Only momentary pacifiers, appetizers are insidious: They appease hunger, then they stimulate it. Again and again.

Such is the life of a wine-baked olive . . . a cherry tomato bonbon . . . an angel on horseback.

Little Cod Beignets

The simplest fish cake you'll ever make, the most ethereal one you'll ever eat. Fresh cod imparts a sweet, meaty taste and a remarkable texture.

1 pound boneless, skinless fresh cod, chilled

2 egg yolks plus 1 egg white, chilled

Peanut oil

Before starting, make sure the fish and eggs are cold. In a food processor, puree the cod until smooth. Add the egg yolks, the egg white, 1 teaspoon salt, and freshly ground white pepper to taste. Process until incorporated. Transfer to a small bowl. Cover and chill 1 hour.

Heat 1 inch of oil in a heavy skillet. Drop the cod puree by rounded teaspoonfuls into the hot fat and fry until brown on both sides, about 5 minutes. Drain on paper towels and keep warm. Sprinkle with salt and serve hot.

Makes 30

ADD-ONS

Throw a handful of curly parsley sprigs (that have been washed and dried) into the hot oil. Fry a few seconds until crisp. Scatter on top of cod fritters. Sprinkle with malt vinegar.

GRAPENOTE

Try with a glass of white Rioja or a crisp fumé blanc from California.

Cherry Tomato Bonbons

Cherry tomatoes attain instant glamour when presented in fancy little paper cups usually reserved for candy. Guests will delight in these one-bite, pop-in-your-mouth savories.

2 dozen small-to-medium cherry tomatoes

1 cup favorite filling:
    Black Olive Tapenade (page 36)
    Lemony Tahina (page 33)
    Eggplant on Fire (page 30)
    Black Hummus (page 35)
    Extra-Bonus Mushroom Pâté (page 38)

⅓ cup freshly chopped curly parsley

Wash the tomatoes and remove any stems. Place stem side down on a cutting board. Slice off the top third of each tomato. With a small spoon (an espresso spoon or a melon baller), scoop out the insides of the tomatoes. Sprinkle the insides lightly with salt and turn upside down on a paper towel to drain.

Turn right-side-up and fill with desired filling, mounding the filling above the rim of the tomatoes. Chill until ready to serve.

Sprinkle with chopped parsley and place each filled tomato in a colorful 1-inch candy paper cup, available at specialty/professional baking stores (page 292). Serve on decorative platter.

Serves 6 to 8

ADD-ONS

You can use more than 1 filling for variety.

GRAPENOTE

Serve with dry sevyal blanc from Clinton Vineyards, New York, or viognier from Preston Vineyards, Sonoma Valley, California.

Eggplant on Fire

Harissa, the fiery red relish of Tunisia and North Africa, adds a pleasurable burn to this cool and smoky eggplant dip. Extinguish the flame with crunchy fresh vegetables or wedges of pita bread.

2½ pounds eggplant (2 very large or 4 medium)

2½ teaspoons harissa (see Note)

3 tablespoons light mayonnaise

Preheat the oven to 400°.

Cook eggplants over an open fire for 2 to 3 minutes on each side until skin is charred and blistered. Place on a baking sheet and bake for 40 minutes. Cut the eggplants in half and let them cool. Scoop out the soft pulp and put it in a bowl.

Add the harissa and mayonnaise. Mash well and add salt and pepper to taste. Refrigerate. You can add more harissa if desired, but taste only when eggplant has chilled and flavors have developed.

Makes 1¾ cups

Note: Harissa can be purchased in small cans or tubes from Middle Eastern and some specialty-food stores (see Sources, page 289).

La Mort du Camembert

Here's an ecologically whimsical way to recycle the box in which good Camembert is invariably packaged: the cheese is baked in its own little wooden "coffin."

1 (8-ounce) Camembert, including box

Fresh sweet herbs, such as lavender or lemon balm

Sliced apples, pears, or grapes

Preheat the oven to 400°.

Peel the wrapping off the cheese. Put the cheese back in the box with a few herbs, cover with the top of the box, and place in the oven. When the cheese begins to melt, remove it from the oven and serve it in the box on a platter surrounded by the fruit.

Serves 4

ADD-ONS

Serve with Twice-Baked Oatcakes (page 32) or thin slices of toasted french bread.

GRAPENOTE

Nice with a California pinot noir, such as Hanley, Calera, or Cuvaison, or with a lighter-style French red Burgundy, like Savigny-les-Beaunes.

Twice-Baked Oatcakes

2¾ cups rolled oats
1 stick unsalted butter, at room temperature, plus 1 tablespoon for greasing pan
½ cup sweetened condensed milk

Preheat the oven to 325°.

Put the oatmeal in a food processor and process until it is the consistency of flour. Put in the bowl of an electric mixer. Add the butter, cut into small pieces, a pinch of salt, and the condensed milk. When well mixed, spread with a flexible metal spatula into a buttered 10- by 6-inch pan or in a 9½-inch tart pan with a removable bottom.

Bake until slightly brown on top and the dough begins to shrink from the sides, about 25 to 30 minutes. Remove and immediately cut into 16 squares or thin wedges. Reduce temperature to 275°. When oven has cooled, put pieces on baking sheet. Bake 12 minutes or until golden. Let cool. The oatcakes keep well in a tin.

Makes 16 pieces

Lemony Tahina

My version of sesame seed sauce—the condiment of choice in the Middle East—is particularly tart and silken. Use as part of a mezze offering—the Levantine answer to antipasto—or toss with strips of steamed chicken and broccoli florets for a special 1-2-3 recipe.

½ cup sesame seed paste (see Note)

2 large lemons

1 large clove garlic

Put the sesame seed paste in the bowl of a food processor. Add the grated zest of 1 lemon and ¼ cup freshly squeezed lemon juice. Add the garlic, pushed through a garlic press.

Start processing, and slowly add ⅓ to ½ cup cold water until you have a smooth, thick puree.

Remove to a bowl. Add salt and freshly ground black pepper to taste and a little more fresh lemon juice, if desire.

Makes 1 cup

ADD-ONS

Serve with Za'atar Pita (page 34) or a basket of crudités for dipping.

Note: Also known as tahini, this is available in jars in specialty-food stores and many supermarkets.

Za'atar Pita

The entire old city of Jerusalem smells of za'atar—an intoxicating blend of hyssop, sesame seeds, and sumac. More intriguing than oregano or basil, za'atar is delightful sprinkled on pita and pizza.

4 pita breads
3 tablespoons extra-virgin olive oil, plus extra for drizzling
¼ cup za'atar

Preheat the oven to 350°.

Lay the pita breads on a baking sheet. Using a pastry brush, spread the oil evenly to cover tops of the pita bread. Sprinkle each with 1 tablespoon za'atar. Drizzle each pita with a little olive oil. Bake 8 minutes, or until the edges just begin to color. Let cool and cut in eighths.

Makes 32 pieces

Black Hummus

Intensely perfumed and ominous-looking, this lentil puree reminds me of hummus—and should similarly be scooped up with lots of pita bread. You must use tiny green French lentils (grown in and exported from Le Puy, France) for the proper texture, taste, and color.

1 cup French green lentils

6 tablespoons black olive puree (tapenade) (see Note)

1 teaspoon Cognac

Pick over and wash the lentils. Put them in a saucepan and cover with 4 cups of water. Add 2 teaspoons salt and 12 whole black peppercorns.

Bring to a full boil, reduce heat, cover, and simmer for 35 minutes, or until the lentils are soft. Drain the lentils, saving ¾ cup cooking liquid. Let cool 15 minutes.

Put the lentils in a food processor with the black olive puree. Process until fairly smooth, adding ½ to ⅓ cup cooking liquid as needed. Remove to a bowl. Add Cognac, and add salt and pepper if needed. Stir well. Cover and refrigerate.

Makes 2½ cups

Notes: You can make your own Black Olive Tapenade (page 36) or buy it ready-made (page 290). Tiny green lentils can be found in specialty-food stores.

Black Olive Tapenade

This Provençal-style olive paste has found a permanent place in America's condiment cabinet. Its lusty, assertive taste adds titillation to a variety of foods, from a basket of crudités to a leg of lamb.

2 cups pitted oil-cured black olives
1 (2-ounce) can anchovies with capers
¼ cup fruity olive oil

Put the olives and anchovies with capers in a food processor or blender. With the motor running, slowly add the oil until the tapenade is smooth; add an extra tablespoon of oil if necessary. Add freshly ground black pepper to taste.

Makes 1¼ cups

ADD-ONS

Add 2 cloves garlic pushed through garlic press and 1 tablespoon fresh lemon juice to the processor after adding the oil.

Sherry Vinegar Mushrooms

Slow, gentle cooking and the verve of sherry vinegar are the secrets of this lip-smacking hors d'oeuvre. Stored in the refrigerator, the mushrooms last for weeks. They won't last for long when brought to room temperature, as there are countless ways to use them.

1 pound large mushrooms (about 18)

½ cup olive oil

2 tablespoons sherry vinegar

Cut the stems off the mushrooms level with the bottom of the cap (leaving the stub of the stem). Beginning at the edge, peel the mushroom caps with your fingers; save the trimmings and the cut stems, which will equal about 1 cup.

Put the mushrooms, stems up, in a nonstick skillet large enough to hold them in a single layer. Pour the olive oil over the mushrooms and sprinkle with 1 teaspoon coarse salt. Cover with a round piece of baking parchment.

Over a very low flame, heat the mushrooms slowly. Cook 5 minutes, turn mushrooms on the other side, and cook 5 minutes. Continue to cook on each side for 4 to 5 minutes, for a total cooking time of 18 to 20 minutes.

Remove the mushrooms with a slotted spoon. Add the vinegar and 12 whole black peppercorns to the juices in pan. Cook over medium heat 2 to 3 minutes. Pour over the mushrooms. Chill.

Serves 6 to 8

Note: Use the reserved trimmings to make Extra-Bonus Mushroom Pâté (page 38).

Note: Use the reserved trimmings to make Extra-Bonus Mushroom Pâté (page 38).

ADD-ONS

Add several sprigs of fresh herbs, such as rosemary or thyme, to the pan juices.

GRAPENOTE

Very appealing with a glass of fino or amontillado sherry.

Extra-Bonus Mushroom Pâté

ADD-ONS

To make crostini:
Spread on thin slices
of toasted French
bread as an hors
d'oeuvre or as an
accompaniment to
soup. Also seductive
spread on top of
sautéed medallions
of filet mignon.

This woodsy spread is wonderful slathered on filet mignon before roasting, stuffed under the skin of a chicken, or simply smoothed onto slices of toasted baguette for humble yet delicious crostini.

1 cup mushroom trimmings (peelings and stems)

2 tablespoons olive oil

2 small cloves garlic, finely chopped

Put all the ingredients in a small, heavy pot with a cover. Cook, covered, over low heat for 25 minutes, or until the mushrooms are very soft. Add salt and freshly ground black pepper to taste. Uncover and cook 1 minute.

Puree in a food processor until smooth. Chill.

Makes ½ cup

Cornmeal-Pasta Chips

More interesting than potato chips, more addictive than popcorn, these too go crackle and crunch. Try them with as many different pasta shapes as you please. Radiatore ("little radiators") are especially habit-forming, if you can find them.

½ pound farfalle (bowtie) pasta or radiatore

½ cup yellow cornmeal

Vegetable oil

Bring salted water to a boil in a large pot. Add the pasta and cook until tender, about 12 minutes. Drain well and pat each piece dry.

In a bowl, mix the cornmeal with ¾ teaspoon salt and freshly ground black pepper. Toss the pasta thoroughly with the cornmeal mixture.

Heat ¼ inch oil in a nonstick skillet. Add the pasta, making sure the pieces don't overlap, and fry 1 to 2 minutes on each side, until crisp and just beginning to get golden brown. Serve warm, sprinkled with additional salt.

Makes one good-size bowlful

ADD-ONS

Sprinkle warm pasta chips with grated parmesan cheese or your favorite spice mixture.

Tiny Pepper Cheese Crackers

On twenty minutes' notice, you can have warm and elegant snacks for friends who drop in. These bracing little bites marry well with a host of thirst quenchers, from iced tea to ice-cold beer.

½ cup plus 3 tablespoons grated Parmigiano-Reggiano cheese

½ cup unsalted butter, at room temperature

1 cup sifted flour

With an electric mixer, cream together ½ cup of the grated cheese and the butter. Mix the flour together with 1 teaspoon salt and 1 teaspoon butcher-grind black pepper. Add to the creamed mixture and blend.

Form into balls ½ inch in diameter, flatten slightly with your palm, and place on an ungreased baking sheet. Sprinkle with remaining cheese. Chill 30 minutes.

Preheat the oven to 450°. Bake the crackers 13 to 14 minutes, until lightly browned.

Makes 30 bite-size crackers

ADD-ONS

Fold ⅓ cup finely chopped pecans into the dough.

GRAPENOTES

Also nice with a glass of chilled sweet vermouth with a lemon twist.

Party Wraps

These attractive little roll-ups pack a flavor wallop in just a few bites. The combinations have been carefully matched for maximum contrast of flavor and texture: bitter radicchio and smoky mozzarella; briny grape leaves and pungent haloumi (a white goat's-milk cheese from Cyprus often flavored with a touch of mint); crisped pancetta and soft boccancini (little mouthfuls of fresh mozzarella). Serve one variety—or a grand platter of them all.

ADD-ONS

Serve with wedges of lemon.

Grape Leaves and Haloumi

12 large grape leaves, packed in brine

8 ounces haloumi cheese, in one piece (see Note)

¼ cup olive oil

Separate the grape leaves and pat each one dry. Cut the cheese into rectangles ⅓ inch thick by 2 inches long by 1 inch wide.

Cut the grape leaves in half from top to stem. Wrap the cheese pieces in the leaves, folding the sides over like an envelope and rolling to cover.

Heat the oil in a nonstick skillet. Sauté the "wraps" on each side until cheese just begins to melt. Place on a platter. Serve warm.

Makes 24 pieces

Note: You can substitute kasseri or firm feta cheese if haloumi is not available.

Radicchio and Smoked Mozzarella

ADD-ONS

Serve with wedges of lemon.

1 large head radicchio

8-ounce piece smoked mozzarella

¼ cup olive oil

Bring salted water to a boil in a large pot. Remove the core from the radicchio and remove any brownish outside leaves. Carefully separate leaves. Place the radicchio in boiling water and cook for 3 to 4 minutes. Put the leaves under cold running water in colander until they cool.

Pat each leaf very dry. Cut the mozzarella into rectangles that are ⅓ inch thick by 2 inches long by 1 inch wide.

Wrap the cheese pieces in radicchio leaves, folding the sides over like an envelope and rolling like a cigar. They will look like stuffed grape leaves.

Heat the oil in a nonstick skillet. Sauté the wraps on each side until the cheese just begins to melt. Place on a platter. Sprinkle with coarse salt and serve warm.

Makes 20 to 24 pieces

Pancetta and Boccancini

8 ounces pancetta, very thinly sliced

1 pound mozzarella cheese or boccancini (see Note)

12 large fresh basil leaves, cut in half lengthwise

If the slices of pancetta are large, cut them in half. Using a 1-inch melon baller, scoop out the mozzarella cheese, or use store-bought boccancini.

Wrap a basil leaf around each cheese ball and wrap a slice of pancetta around the basil. Secure with a toothpick or wooden skewer that has been soaked in water for 30 minutes.

Preheat the broiler. Put wraps on the broiler rack and broil 3 to 4 minutes on each side, until pancetta is crisp. Serve hot.

Makes 18

Note: Boccancini are small "mouthfuls" of mozzarella cheese formed into balls approximately ¾ inch in diameter.

Lacquered Chicken Wings

Incredibly good but oh, so sticky; you might consider finger bowls for your guests. Slow baking creates a mahogany glaze, sealing in the sweet and salty flavors that characterize much of Asian cookery.

12 large chicken wings

½ cup dark soy sauce

½ cup packed dark brown sugar

Preheat the oven to 350°.

Cut off the wing tips with a sharp, heavy knife and discard. Cut wings into two pieces, separating them at the joint.

Place the wings in a shallow roasting pan. Combine the soy sauce and sugar and a liberal grinding of black pepper and pour the mixture over the chicken, coating it well. Let marinate 30 minutes.

Bake for 30 minutes. Remove the pan from the oven and turn each piece with tongs. (For a more elegant look, transfer wings to a wire rack at this point in the recipe.) Bake an additional 30 minutes. Turn again and bake 15 minutes longer. The wings will be a rich dark brown and very tender. Serve on a platter.

Makes 24 pieces

ADD-ONS

Sprinkle with rice vinegar before serving. Or scatter toasted sesame seeds on top.

GRAPENOTE

How about sake on ice with a long, thin strip of cucumber?

Med-Rim Lamb Nuggets, I and II

In Arabic cultures these aromatic nuggets would be known as kefta: a mixture of ground lamb (or beef) with spices and flavorings, formed into balls, sausages, or long, thin "snakes." On skewers, they're called kefta kebabs.

I

8 ounces ground lamb

1 large clove garlic, pushed through a garlic press

½ teaspoon ground cumin

II

8 ounces ground lamb

½ tablespoon dried mint

2 tablespoons freshly minced onion

Put the ground lamb, the spices of your choice, 1 tablespoon cold water, ½ teaspoon salt, and freshly ground black pepper in a medium bowl. Mix well with your hands. Roll between your palms to make oval shapes 1¼ inches long by ¾ inch wide.

Preheat the broiler. Place the lamb nuggets on a baking sheet or pie tin and broil 5 minutes. Serve hot.

I, II: Makes 14 to 15 nuggets for 8 ounces of lamb

Angels and Archangels on Horseback

Often used as a "savory" in traditional English menus, Angels on Horseback are served at the end of the meal, after the sweet, to neutralize the sugar taste before port is served. When scallops are substituted, the dish is known as Archangels on Horseback. (Archangels are angels of particularly high rank.) In America they make great party food.

ADD-ONS

You can spread the warm toasts with anchovy paste. A whole flat parsley leaf looks splendid on each scallop.

GRAPENOTE

These heavenly morsels calls for a good brut Champagne.

6 to 8 slices of brioche loaf or thin white bread, crusts removed

2 dozen fresh oysters or sea scallops

12 slices of bacon

Preheat the oven to 450°.

Cut 1½-inch circles out of the bread; you should have 24. Toast lightly on both sides in the oven (about 7 minutes total). Reserve.

Pat the oysters or scallops dry with paper towels.

Cut the bacon strips in half and wrap each strip around an oyster or scallop. Secure tightly with toothpicks.

Place in a baking pan. Bake the oysters for 10 minutes, scallops for 12 minutes. Remove the picks and serve on the toasts.

Makes 24

Fried Chickpeas with Sage and Walnut Oil

This is my husband's favorite party food, but he likes these equally well strewn over a piece of char-grilled swordfish. We first tried these crunchy beans with crisp bits of fried sage somewhere near Frontière—where Italy meets France. Use freshly cooked chickpeas for the best texture.

2 cups cooked chickpeas (see Note)

3 tablespoons walnut oil

1½ tablespoons dried sage leaves (see Note)

Use freshly cooked or canned chickpeas. Drain well and pat completely dry.

In a medium-size nonstick skillet, heat the oil. When the oil is hot but not smoking, add the chickpeas and fry until they get crisp (they should be crisp on the outside, creamy on the inside). Add the sage leaves and ½ teaspoon coarse salt. Continue to cook 1 to 2 minutes. Drizzle with a little more walnut oil if the chickpeas look dry.

Let cool a few minutes before serving with drinks. Provide lots of napkins.

To serve as a side dish, add a few tablespoons of water and simmer, covered, 2 minutes. Drizzle with a little walnut oil.

Makes 2 cups

Notes: To cook chickpeas: Soak 8 ounces overnight in cold water. Drain, cover with water, and cook about 2 hours, or until tender.

You can buy whole dried sage leaves in specialty-food stores, Middle Eastern stores, or spice stores (see Sources, page 289). Spice Islands also packages good-quality dried sage leaves, available in your supermarket.

Rosettes of Smoked Salmon on Cucumber Rounds

ADD-ONS

Put a sprig of fresh dill in the center of each rosette. Serve on a bed of thinly sliced lemons.

GRAPENOTE

Serve with a salmon-hued rosé champagne—a Billecart-Salmon, perhaps? Or try one from Dom Ruinart.

One of the most popular hors d'oeuvre at the Rainbow Room, these roses are elegant and edible. Use a hothouse cucumber for a seedless and uniform base. Serve on a crystal platter garnished with garden-variety roses—salmon-colored, of course.

**1 hothouse cucumber, or 2 regular cucumbers
(long and thin, about 1½ inches in diameter)**

8 ounces very thinly sliced smoked salmon

½ cup whipped cream cheese

Wash the cucumbers. Do not peel them. Cut them into thin circles, ¼ inch thick, and pat dry. There should be about 24 slices.

Slice the smoked salmon into strips 1 inch wide by 3 inches long, making about 24 pieces. Roll loosely. Curl back the edges and flatten slightly so that it begins to look like a rose. Spread about 1 teaspoon of cream cheese on each cucumber slice and place rosette on top.

If desired, fill the center of each "rosette" with about ½ teaspoon whipped cream cheese. Arrange on a platter.

Makes 24

Parmesan Lace Galettes

These miraculous, delicate disks are simply fashioned from melted cheese. Delicious warm or at room temperature, they stay crisp and translucent. If you want to feel like a three-star chef, garnish salads and fish dishes with a galette. In Italy these are known as frico croccante.

> 4 tablespoons unsalted butter
>
> 1 cup grated good-quality Parmesan cheese
>
> 2 teaspoons fennel seeds, cumin seeds, or
>   caraway seeds

In an 8-inch nonstick skillet, melt ½ tablespoon of the butter over low heat. Let it get foamy but not brown.

Coat the bottom of the skillet with ¼ cup of the grated cheese. Sprinkle evenly with ½ teaspoon fennel, cumin, or caraway seeds. Pack down with a spatula and let the cheese melt slowly and begin to brown and harden. Flip the galette over, adding 1½ teaspoons butter to pan. Let the cheese get golden brown on other side. This will take about 4 to 5 minutes on the first side, 2 to 3 minutes on the second side. The galette will be crisp. Remove the galette from the skillet to paper towels. Repeat the process three more times, using the same amounts of butter and cheese.

Serve warm with cocktails, or as a dramatic garnish for main courses and salads.

Makes 4 galettes, 6 inches in diameter

Ouzo Feta Spread

"Mezedes," little dishes of food customarily served with drinks, form the basis of social life in Greece. They are served in neighborhood "ouzeries"—pubs that feature ouzo (a clear, fiery, licorice-flavored alcohol) and appetizers such as this one.

Add-Ons

Serve with warm pita bread or Flying Saucers (page 55) and fresh cucumber spears.

12 ounces feta cheese, in one piece

3 tablespoons extra-virgin olive oil

1 tablespoon ouzo (see Note)

Soak the block of feta in a bowl with cold water to cover for 30 minutes. Remove from the water and pat dry.

Crumble the cheese into the bowl of a food processor. Begin to process the cheese and slowly add the olive oil. Blend until completely smooth. Add the ouzo and some freshly ground black pepper. Process until incorporated.

Chill 2 hours. Drizzle with a little olive oil before serving.

Makes 1½ cups

Note: You can use another licorice-flavored liqueur, such as anisette, sambuca, or pernod.

Wine-Baked Olives

For wine enthusiasts who think "life is a cabernet," here's a creative use for bottom-of-the-bottle leftovers. Baked in rich red wine, olives become fleshy and voluptuous.

> **1 pound kalamata olives**
>
> **½ cup dry red wine (a cabernet)**
>
> **¼ cup extra-virgin olive oil or Garlic Oil (page 52)**

Preheat the oven to 350°.

Put the olives in a small saucepan and cover with water. Bring to a boil and boil for 1 minute. Drain well in a colander.

In a small ovenproof, nonmetallic dish, put olives, wine, and olive oil or Garlic Oil.

Bake 30 minutes, turning once during baking. Serve warm or at room temperature. Much of the liquid will have evaporated.

Makes 1 pound (about 85)

Garlic Oil

16 medium-to-large cloves garlic
2 cups olive oil
2 California bay leaves

Peel the garlic and place in oil in small, heavy enamel pot. Heat gently 5 minutes, or until bubbles form on top. Turn off heat. Add the bay leaves and ½ teaspoon whole black peppercorns. Let steep and let cool. The garlic oil will last two weeks in the refrigerator.

Makes 2 cups

THE FOLLOWING PHOTOS DEPICT:

Party Food and Appetizers:

1. Cherry Tomato Bonbons
2. Party Wraps:
    Radicchio and Smoked Mozzarella
    Grape Leaves and Haloumi
3. Rosettes of Smoked Salmon on Cucumber Rounds
4. Lacquered Chicken Wings

First Courses:

5. Shrimp with a Kiss
6. Celery Rémoulade, Celeriac Chips; Roasted Red Peppers,
    Yellow Pepper Puree; Salad of Roasted Beets and Beet Greens, Walnut Oil
7. Seared Sea Scallops on Sweet Pea Puree
8. Tomato, Mozzarella, and Basil: Six Styles

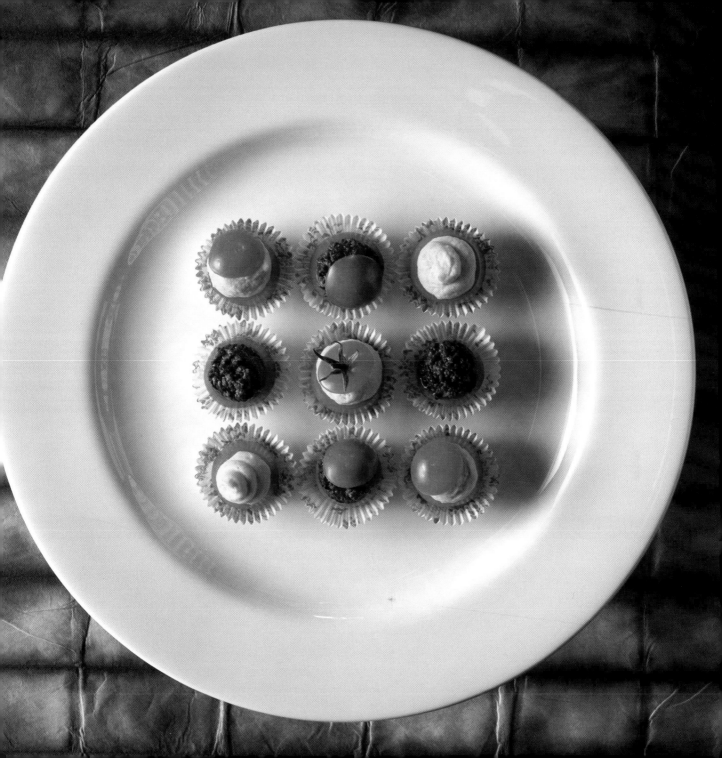

Venetian Wafers

A crisp, flavorful snack to accompany a glass of sparkling wine, this is a quick study of textural contrasts: cold bubbles cut through warm richness. Dream of the Piazza San Marco and the Grand Canal.

> 24 slices sopressata salami, 3 inches in diameter
>
> ½ cup grated good-quality Parmesan cheese
>
> 2 tablespoons fennel seeds

Preheat the oven to 500°.

Place sopressata on a large baking sheet. Put 1 teaspoon cheese on top of each slice of sopressata to cover evenly. Sprinkle each with fennel.

Bake 5 minutes. Remove from the oven and serve while still warm. Wafers will be crisp.

Makes 24 wafers

GRAPENOTE

Drink a glass of chilled prosecco, the dry sparkling wine of the Veneto region.

Brillat-Savarin's Fondue

ADD-ONS

Serve with slices of a good-quality baguette, lightly toasted, rubbed with a garlic clove. Grilled Shiitake Mushrooms, Garlic Essence (page 76), go well with this fondue and together make an exciting meal.

GRAPENOTE

"Call for the best wine, which will be copiously drunk, and you will see miracles." Quote is from M.F.K. Fisher's adaptation of Brillat-Savarin's *The Physiology of Taste*, 1986.

Not like any fondue you've had before, this version offered by the revered gastronome Anthelme Brillat-Savarin in The Physiology of Taste *(1825) is somewhere between molten cheese sauce and soft scrambled eggs.*

His recipe went like this: "Weigh the number of eggs you wish to use, according to the presumed number of your guests. Then take a piece of good Gruyère cheese weighing one-third of this amount, and a morsel of butter weighing one-sixth of it." My version follows.

6 eggs

4 ounces Gruyère cheese

4 tablespoons (½ stick) unsalted butter, plus additional butter for coating casserole

Beat the eggs well. Cut the cheese and butter in small cubes. Pour all into a buttered flameproof casserole or a buttered 12-inch oval gratin pan.

"Put the casserole on a lively fire, and turn the contents with a spatula, until they have become properly thick and soft; add a little salt, or none at all according to whether the cheese is old or not, and a good amount of pepper, which is one of the characteristics of this time-honored dish; serve it on a gently heated platter."

Serves 4

Flying Saucers

Serendipity in the kitchen led to this amazing transformation of flour and oil into light, fluffy Frisbees of fried bread served hot from the skillet.

1 cup sifted flour

2 tablespoons plus ¼ cup olive oil

2 scallions, trimmed and sliced thin, about ⅓ cup

Sift together the flour and ½ teaspoon salt. Put the flour mixture in the bowl of an electric mixer. Make a well in the center and add ¼ cup warm water and the 2 tablespoons olive oil. With the paddle attachment, mix until a dough forms and knead 6 to 7 minutes, until dough is smooth and satiny.

Add the scallions and mix for just a few seconds longer; overmixing will make the dough sticky.

Divide the dough into 4 balls. Roll out each on a lightly floured surface to a diameter of 6 inches and a thickness of ¼ inch.

(You can roll the pancakes out as long as 3 hours prior to cooking, separating them with paper towels and then wrapping the stack in plastic wrap.)

Heat the remaining ¼ cup oil in an 8-inch skillet and fry the circles of dough, one at a time, until golden brown on both sides. Keep them warm while you finish making all of them. Cut into triangles and serve immediately.

Serves 8

ADD-ONS

For an interesting first course, place a mound of julienned arugula on top of each flying saucer. Drizzle with Lemon Vinaigrette (page 56) and a dash of freshly ground black pepper. Serve with a fork and knife.

GRAPENOTE

Serve with a chilled California riesling, such as Jekel, Geyser Peak, or Hop Kiln. Or try an Alsatian pinot blanc from Leon Beyer or Pierre Sparr.

Lemon Vinaigrette

A lovely and refreshing splash for green salads mixed with lots of herbs and tossed with freshly cooked legumes (white beans or trendy borlotti, or cranberry, beans) or steamed vegetables (carrots, broccoli, leaves of brussels sprouts).

> **1 teaspoon Dijon mustard**
> **3 tablespoons fresh lemon juice**
> **½ cup extra-virgin olive oil**

Whisk together the mustard and the lemon juice. Slowly whisk in the olive oil, a little at a time, until emulsified. Season with ½ teaspoon coarse salt and freshly ground white pepper.

Makes ⅔ cup

Chapter 7

First Courses

*T*he notion of a first course has changed over the years.

What once were the first-course mandates—grapefruit maraschino, iced cherrystones, alligator pear, and turtle soup—have given way to anarchy-on-a-plate: nachos grandes, foie gras nuggets, and main-courses-in-miniature.

However difficult they may be to define today, many of us opt for two or three and call it dinner.

Salmon Carpaccio Cooked on a Plate

Gerard Pangaud, our chef at Restaurant Aurora in New York, gained fame in Paris for cooking food directly on a dinner plate placed in an ultra-hot oven. This "flash-heat" method produces the most natural tastes and satiny textures. Be sure to use a heat-resistant plate!

1-pound piece fresh salmon fillet, cut from the center of the fish

2 tablespoons green peppercorns, drained (see Note)

Extra-virgin olive oil

Remove the skin and with tweezers remove all the little bones from the salmon. Freeze 15 minutes, or until very cold. This will make it easier to slice.

Slice the salmon very thin on an extreme angle, as if it were smoked salmon. Put the slices between sheets of waxed paper and press down with the heel of your hand to flatten.

Preheat the oven to 500°.

Arrange the slices in one layer, not overlapping, to cover the surface of six 9-inch ovenproof plates. Season with a little coarse salt, freshly ground white pepper, 1 teaspoon green peppercorns, and several teaspoons of oil. Let sit 15 minutes.

Put the plates in the oven for 2 to 3 minutes to warm the salmon, but do not let it cook through. Serve immediately, handling the plates with a pot holder.

Serves 6

Note: Green peppercorns come in small cans, packed in brine, available in supermarkets and specialty-food stores.

ADD-ONS

Sprinkle some fresh lemon juice over the top.

GRAPENOTE

Open a bottle of buttery chardonnay from California, from Kistler, Acacia, or Carneros Creek. Or try a vintage Krug champagne with some bottle age.

Salad of Roasted Beets and Beet Greens, Walnut Oil

How considerate of the beet to provide two vegetables in one, edible leaves and a thick, fleshy root. This gorgeous salad is enhanced by the sophisticated coupling of walnut oil and fresh lemon. Pass the pepper mill and some warm dinner rolls.

> 2 bunches of medium-to-large beets, with beet tops
>
> ⅓ cup walnut oil
>
> 3 tablespoons fresh lemon juice

Preheat the oven to 400°.

Cut the leafy greens off the beets and save them. Trim and wash the beets but do not peel them. Put them in a shallow casserole with ¼ inch of water and bake 1½ hours. Add a little more water during baking. When the beets are tender, a knife will penetrate them easily; remove from the oven and let cool. Peel with a sharp knife. Cut the beets into 1½- by ¼-inch batons.

Put the beets in a bowl and toss with 1 tablespoon walnut oil and 1 tablespoon lemon juice. Sprinkle with salt. Keep at room temperature.

Bring a large pot of salted water to a boil. Wash the beet greens well and break them into large pieces. Add the greens to the pot and cook 5 minutes, or until tender.

Drain well. Let cool and toss with remaining walnut oil and lemon juice. Add salt and freshly ground black pepper to taste. Serve greens on a platter, scattered with cooked beet "batons."

Serves 4 to 6

ADD-ONS

Top with warm freshly cooked bacon that is barely crisp and coarsely crumbled. Or add walnuts that have been lightly toasted.

GRAPENOTE

Because there is a minimum of acid, this salad does nicely with wine. Try a chenin blanc or semillon, or a fruity rosé like a rosé of zinfandel from Pedroncelli or from Green and Red.

Shrimp with a Kiss

When you suck the tender meat from these crusty crustacean shells, you make wonderful little noises that sound like slurpy kisses. "Col bacio" in Italian, this dish was inspired by Marcella Hazan.

> **2 pounds medium-large shrimp in their shells (20–24 per pound)**
>
> **1 cup dry bread crumbs**
>
> **⅔ cup Garlic Oil (page 52) plus extra for drizzling**

Pat shrimp dry. Leave the shells intact but remove the small legs with scissors. If using smaller shrimp, slip a toothpick under the shells running the length of the shrimp to keep them straight.

Put the shrimp in a bowl with ⅔ cup of the oil, and a liberal amount of coarse salt and butcher-grind black pepper. Marinate at room temperature for 1 hour.

Preheat the broiler. Toss the shrimp with the bread crumbs, place in a shallow baking pan and broil close to the heat for 1 to 2 minutes on each side. Shells will be slightly charred. Sprinkle with additional coarse salt and drizzle with 2 tablespoons garlic oil.

Serves 6

ADD-ONS

Serve with lemon wedges and an abundance of paper napkins.

GRAPENOTE

This dish requires a bold white of considerable heft, like a Sanford chardonnay from California.

Arugula and Mussel Salad, Anchovy Vinaigrette

This dish tastes and smells of the deep blue sea. "Liquor" from the mussels softens the anchovies' intensity, while arugula adds a refreshing peppery note. Use plump green-lipped mussels from New Zealand if you can find them.

1 pound fresh medium-size cultivated mussels in shells

2 bunches arugula

1 (2-ounce) can anchovies with capers

Wash the mussels well in a colander. Beard if necessary. Do not dry the mussels. Transfer them to a heavy pot. Add ¼ cup water, cover the pot tightly, and cook over low heat, shaking the pot occasionally. The mussels will open in 3 to 4 minutes. Remove from the heat, uncover, and let the mussels cool. Remove the mussels from their shells and reserve the cooking liquid.

Thoroughly wash the arugula. Dry well and keep chilled.

Put the anchovies with capers and the oil from the can in a blender and puree until smooth. Add 2 to 3 tablespoons mussel liquid and some freshly ground black pepper. Toss the arugula with the cooled mussels. Pour just enough dressing over the salad to coat the leaves lightly, and toss.

Serves 4

ADD-ONS

Add 2 teaspoons balsamic vinegar to the blender, or pass a cruet of vinegar at the table. Colorful and delicious with wedges of hard-boiled eggs.

GRAPENOTE

Try a chenin blanc from the Loire Valley or a more earthy Gavi, from Italy.

Farmhouse Cheddar Frittata

Thick, flat omelets served hot or at room temperature can be found in Spain as tortillas *and in Italy as* frittate. *Hybrid flavors like sharp English farmhouse Cheddar and spicy, pickled jalapeños make this preparation decidedly global.*

12 ounces English farmhouse Cheddar

½ cup sliced pickled jalapeños from a jar, reserving 2 tablespoons liquid

10 extra-large eggs

Preheat the oven to 350°.

Grate the cheese on the largest holes of a box grater. Reserve.

Pat the jalapeño slices dry with paper towels. Spray a 10-inch springform pan with a removable bottom with vegetable spray. Scatter the jalapeños evenly on the bottom of the pan. Sprinkle the cheese evenly on top.

Put the eggs, ½ teaspoon salt, and a pinch of white pepper in the bowl of an electric mixer. Mix on medium speed for 4 minutes, or until very light. Add the 2 tablespoons reserved juice and mix.

Pour the eggs over the cheese in the pan. Place the pan on a baking sheet and bake for 20 to 25 minutes. Let cool 10 minutes before serving.

Serves 6 to 8 as a first course, 16 as hors d'oeuvre

ADD-ONS

Serve with Roasted Red Peppers, Yellow Pepper Puree (page 68), for a delightful lunch. Or serve a smaller portion, garnished with a tuft of wild greens dressed with a simple vinaigrette, as a first course.

GRAPENOTE

I like beer with this, particularly Celis White, a Belgian-style beer wheat from Texas.

Iceberg Hearts, Bacon, and Blue Cheese Dressing

An homage to the past, when iceberg was at the heart of all salads. An iceberg tip: Slam the bottom of the head on a wooden board and the core will simply fall out.

8 ounces blue cheese

1 large head iceberg lettuce

8 slices bacon, cooked crisp and kept warm

Break the blue cheese into chunks and place it in a food processor. Process the cheese while adding 7 tablespoons cold water, a little at a time. Blend until completely smooth. Add some freshly ground black pepper. Chill until ready to use. Makes 1 cup. If you like your dressing chunky, add ⅓ cup more crumbled blue cheese.

Cut the lettuce into 6 wedges. Pour blue cheese dressing over the top. Crumble the bacon into large pieces and sprinkle it over the tops of the lettuce wedges. Serve on chilled plates and pass the pepper mill.

Serves 6

ADD-ONS

Add a small clove of garlic, pushed through a garlic press, to the blue cheese dressing.

Swedish Cured Salmon

On any Swedish smorgasbord, once known as "the vodka table," you invariably find two or three preparations of gravlax—a curing, not a smoking, of whole sides of succulent salmon. Do as the Swedes do: Serve hot creamed potatoes as an accompaniment. Drink "snaps" (chilled vodka or flavored aquavit), with beer on the side.

3 pounds side of salmon, preferably the center cut

¼ cup sugar

1½ cups freshly chopped dill, stems included

Remove all the small bones from the salmon with tweezers. Pat the fish dry. Rub the salmon flesh with ¼ cup kosher salt, 1 tablespoon butcher-grind black pepper, the sugar, and the chopped dill. Cover with plastic wrap. Weight down with a brick or other heavy object and refrigerate 48 to 72 hours.

Before serving, scrape off the dill and seasonings. Slice on the bias as if it were smoked salmon.

Serves 8 to 10

ADD-ONS

Delicious served with hot Creamed Potatoes Swedish-Style (page 201). You can also grill 6-ounce portions and serve them medium-rare.

GRAPENOTES

Serve with small glasses of ice-cold aquavit or vodka.

Sweet Mustard Sauce

It's funny how deprivation sometimes leads to discovery. With only three ingredients to play with, I left out the oil and egg generally used in making traditional Swedish mustard sauce for gravlax, shrimp, and herring. And guess what?

   3 tablespoons sugar
   2 tablespoons distilled white vinegar
   ¼ cup Dijon mustard

Put the sugar and vinegar in a small bowl and stir until the sugar dissolves. Whisk in the mustard thoroughly with a wire whisk. Sauce will thicken.

Makes ½ cup

Bresaola and Asiago "Carpaccio," Truffle Oil

ADD-ONS

You can roll the bresaola around a filling of arugula to make a roulade. Add shards of cheese and drizzle with truffle oil.

GRAPENOTE

Go Italian all the way, from a fruity Dolcetto to a more woodsy Spanna or Gattinara.

Heady flavors come together for an ultra-chic first course. Bresaola, air-dried beef from northern Italy, has an intense, gamy taste, while Asiago, cow's-milk cheese from the Veneto, has a rich, nutty flavor ending with a sharp note. With just a few drops of sensuous truffle oil, Carpaccio (a sixteenth-century Venetian painter) would surely have a satisfied palate! If you can't find bresaola, substitute Bündnerfleisch, which is air-dried cured beef from Austria or Switzerland.

8 ounces thinly sliced bresaola

3 ounces young Asiago cheese

1 tablespoon truffle oil (see Sources, page 291)

Cover 6 large plates with thinly sliced bresaola. Wrap tightly with plastic wrap until ready to use.

Using a mandoline, a very sharp knife, or a cheese slicer, cut paper-thin slices of cheese. Scatter the cheese in the center of the bresaola. Drizzle with truffle oil and sprinkle with coarse salt and butcher-grind black pepper.

Serves 6

Celery Rémoulade, Celeriac Chips

Celery rémoulade is part of every Paris bistro's hors d'oeuvre variés. France's mustardy answer to coleslaw, it is made with a variety of celery grown for its turnip-like root. My version adds unexpected crisps of roasted celeriac.

1½ pounds celery root (celeriac)

½ cup plus 2 tablespoons light mayonnaise

3 tablespoons Dijon mustard

Preheat the oven to 400°.

Wash the celery root and peel. Cut two-thirds of the celery root into very thin julienne strips, about 2 inches long.

Mix the mayonnaise and mustard together in a bowl and add the julienned celery root. Add salt and pepper to taste. Mix well and refrigerate.

Slice the remaining third of the celery root paper-thin. Place the slices on a baking sheet, reduce the heat to 275°, and bake, turning once or twice, 30 minutes, or until crisp. The celery root chips will brown lightly, but do not let them get too dark.

Sprinkle with salt. Serve a mound of celery rémoulade with celery root chips on top.

Serves 5 to 6

ADD-ONS

Serve the salad on a bed of thinly sliced prosciutto or "speck," which is smoked prosciutto.

Roasted Red Peppers, Yellow Pepper Puree

ADD-ONS

Serve with a cruet of vinegar: red wine, balsamic, or Herbes de Provence (page 69).

GRAPENOTE

A mouth-filling, fruity chardonnay would do nicely; as would a white Meritage blend from Carmenet, in California.

If forced to pick my favorite vegetable, I'd choose a roasted pepper. Sweet and meaty, it adds sex appeal to many dishes. But here it takes center stage, a red one against a backdrop of yellow pepper puree.

6 large red bell peppers

4 large yellow bell peppers

½ cup extra-virgin olive oil or Garlic Oil (page 52)

Hold the whole peppers over an open flame or place in the broiler, turning periodically, until skins get very black on all sides. This will take 10 to 15 minutes in the broiler.

Put the peppers in a brown paper bag and seal the bag to steam them. Let the peppers get cool enough to handle and peel the skins from the peppers. Core all the peppers but keep the red peppers whole, taking out the seeds from the center. Put aside.

Cut the yellow peppers into strips, removing all the seeds. Puree the strips in a blender with the oil until creamy and emulsified. Add coarse salt and freshly ground black pepper.

To serve, spoon yellow pepper puree on the plates and top with the red peppers. Sprinkle with sea salt.

Serves 6

Herbes de Provence Vinegar

2 cups red wine vinegar
2 teaspoons dried herbes de provence (see Note)
1 long sprig of fresh rosemary

Combine all the ingredients in a small enamel saucepan with ½ teaspoon whole black peppercorns. Bring to a boil, turn off the heat, and let cool. Put in a jar with the herbs and cover tightly. Store in a cool, dark place.

Makes 2 cups

Note: Available in specialty-food or spice stores (see Sources, page 289).

Veal Sausage with Asparagus Sauce and Asparagus Tips

GRAPENOTE

A white wine and a red wine will take this dish in two very different directions: A good warm-weather choice would be New Zealand's prized Cloudy Bay sauvignon blanc or the less pricey Stoneleigh; for cooler days try an elegant Sancerre Rouge from the Loire.

No one will believe that this dish, striking to look at and to taste, has only three ingredients. Use best-quality weisswurst from your gourmet shop, although in a pinch supermarket bratwurst (a combination of veal and pork) will suffice.

1 pound fresh thin asparagus

1½ cups homemade chicken broth (page 96) or canned

4 to 5 fat veal sausages, weisswurst or bratwurst (1½ pounds)

Cut the tips off the asparagus stalks and reserve the tips for later use. Snap off the woody bottoms of the asparagus stems and discard. Cut the remainder of each stalk into thirds.

Put the asparagus pieces and chicken broth in an enamel saucepan and cook over medium heat for 15 minutes, or until tender. Transfer the asparagus and broth to a blender. Puree 2 or 3 minutes, until sauce is very smooth. Makes 2 cups.

Steam the sausages over boiling water for 8 to 10 minutes, or boil them for 5 minutes. Keep them warm.

Gently heat the asparagus sauce.

Blanch the asparagus tips in boiling water for 2 to 3 minutes. Drain.

Slice the sausages ½ inch thick on the bias, place on a pool of sauce, and scatter with the asparagus tips.

Serves 4 or 5

Pan-Roast Oysters with Butter and Leeks

"Palatable indulgence," said the great food writer Lucullus about the oyster. What would he have said about this dish? I say, Perfection, with a nice buttery chardonnay.

½ cup (1 stick) unsalted butter

2 pints fresh oysters, shucked, juice reserved

1 bunch leeks

Preheat the oven to 400°.

Use some of the butter to grease a shallow baking dish. Place the oysters in the dish. Melt the remaining butter in large nonstick skillet. Reserve.

Trim the leeks, saving the white part only. Cut in half lengthwise, wash well, and pat dry. Julienne the leeks and add to the melted butter. Cook slowly for 15 minutes; then add ¼ cup of the reserved oyster juice, salt to taste, and 2 teaspoons whole black peppercorns.

Pour the leek mixture over the oysters and bake about 10 minutes, or until the edges begin to curl. Serve immediately.

Serves 4 to 6

ADD-ONS

Serve with Tiny Pepper Cheese Crackers (page 40). Add ½ cup heavy cream to the pan juices and then a few tablespoons of dry vermouth. Serve in soup plates.

GRAPENOTE

A great match with a Puligny Montrachet, or the less expensive Rully.

Checkerboard Orzo Salad

Meticulously cut cubes of red tomatoes and firm white ricotta salata in this recipe remind me of a checkerboard—or of those charming checkered tablecloths found in trattorias. Equally homey is this refreshing conjunction of flavors and textures.

1 pound medium-size ripe tomatoes

6 ounces ricotta salata, in one piece

8 ounces uncooked orzo pasta

Carefully cut the tomatoes into neat little ⅓-inch cubes and put the cubes in a shallow bowl. Cut the ricotta salata into the same size cubes. Add to tomatoes with a sprinkling of coarse salt and freshly ground black pepper. Let sit 1 hour.

Bring a medium-size pot of salted water to a boil. Add the orzo and cook until tender, about 10 minutes. Drain. Put the orzo in a medium-size bowl and add half of the tomato-cheese mixture, along with any juices that have collected in the bottom of the bowl. Toss gently, adding salt to taste.

Put the orzo mixture on a platter and top with the remaining tomato-cheese mixture. Serve warm or at room temperature.

Serves 4

ADD-ONS

Toss the tomato-cheese mixture with ½ tablespoon fresh thyme leaves.

Niçoise Socca Crêpe, Marinated Goat Cheese

Socca, a kind of pizza made from chickpea flour, is an omnipresent snack in Nice. Here it's gone upscale with trendy goat cheese marinated in fruity, green olive oil. Use a domestic cheese from Coach Farms or Laura Chenel, or French Montrachet. Speaking of Montrachet, a glass of this chilled white Burgundy is an impressive partner.

> 8 thick slices of goat cheese, cut 1 inch thick (Coach Farms, or Laura Chenel, or Montrachet)
>
> ⅓ cup plus ⅓ cup extra-virgin olive oil or Garlic Oil (page 52)
>
> 1 cup chickpea flour (see Sources, page 290)

Put the cheese in large shallow bowl or plate. Pour the ⅓ cup oil over the top and sprinkle lightly with coarse salt. Let marinate 1 hour.

Sift the chickpea flour into a mixing bowl. Make a well and whisk in ½ cup water to form a smooth, thick paste. Add another ½ cup water, 2 tablespoons olive or garlic oil, ¼ teaspoon coarse salt, and a grinding of black pepper. Stir until very smooth.

Heat an 8-inch nonstick skillet until hot. Coat the bottom with 1 teaspoon olive oil. When it starts smoking, pour in a 2-ounce ladle of batter to cover the bottom evenly.

When the batter has set, turn over, adding a little more oil, and cook other side until golden. Remove to warm plates. Turn out onto a warm plate and repeat with the remaining batter to make 8 crêpes.

To serve, top each crêpe with marinated cheese.

Serves 8

A great Montrachet or a full-bodied California chardonnay are perfect mates. A chilled Chiroubles from Beaujolais or a lighter-style pinot noir from California will be easier on the pocketbook.

Asparagus and Prosciutto Bundles, Melted Fontina

ADD-ONS

Instead of melted fontina, use hot poached eggs.

GRAPENOTE

A glass of a medium-bodied, grassy sauvignon blanc would be good for hard-to-match asparagus and a wonderful way to begin your meal. If the wine has a bit of residual sugar, it will play off the salty perfume of the prosciutto.

A member of the lily family, asparagus comes in three varieties: white, green, and violet. Wrapped in a blanket of pink prosciutto, these are edible bundles of joy. Swathe them in a sauce of Italian fontina for a strong, nutty taste.

1 pound medium-size asparagus

4 ounces thinly sliced prosciutto

6 ounces Italian fontina cheese

Snap off the woody ends of the asparagus. Lightly scrape the stalks of the asparagus with a vegetable peeler.

Bring a pot of salted water to a boil. Add the asparagus and cook 8 to 10 minutes, until tender. With tongs, transfer the asparagus to a bowl of ice water to retain the bright green color. Let sit 5 minutes. Remove the asparagus and pat dry with paper towels.

Make 4 to 6 bundles of 5 to 6 asparagus each. Wrap each bundle with 2 slices of prosciutto, making a large pink band.

Cut the cheese into 1-inch pieces. In a small, heavy saucepan, heat 2 tablespoons water. Add the cheese and stir with a wooden spoon until completely melted. When ready to serve, place bundles under the broiler for 1 minute to warm. Quickly spoon cheese over asparagus bundles.

Serves 4 to 6

Mesclun and Blood Orange Salad, Orange Vinaigrette

In the late 1980s, fancy wild greens became de rigueur in the best restaurants. Luckily for us, mesclun—an inventive mix of lettuces that includes frisée, radicchio, red oakleaf, mâche, and, occasionally, edible flowers—is now available in many food markets. Substitute flavorful Valencia oranges if blood oranges are not in season.

6 ounces mesclun (variety of mixed greens)

4 large blood oranges

¼ cup extra-virgin olive oil—plus additional for drizzling, if desired

Wash the lettuce and dry it completely. Reserve.

Grate the zest of 1 orange to make ½ teaspoon. Squeeze 1 to 2 oranges so you have ¼ cup juice.

In a small bowl, whisk together the orange juice, orange zest, and olive oil and season with ¼ teaspoon coarse salt and some freshly ground black pepper.

Remove the rind from the remaining oranges with a small, sharp knife. Cut in between the membranes to separate the orange segments and remove all membrane.

Pile the lettuce high on large chilled plates. Tuck the orange segments in and around the lettuce and spoon the dressing over the salad. If desired, drizzle additional olive oil around the edge of the salad.

Serves 4 or 5

Grilled Shiitake Mushrooms, Garlic Essence

ADD-ONS

Serve warm as a
first course over
White Polenta with
Parmigiano-Reggiano
(page 189), or cold as
a salad with Roasted
Red Peppers, Yellow
Pepper Puree (page
68). Scatter sprigs of
fresh thyme or
rosemary over the
mushrooms while
baking.

GRAPENOTES

"Big" and "bold" are
the operative words:
try a smoky fume
blanc reserve from
Mondavi, or full-
bodied chardonnay
from Rosemount
Estate, in Australia,
or Zaca Mesa or
Murphy-Goode from
California. Look for
the words "barrel-
fermented,"
"barrel-aged," or
"reserve" on the label.

Unbeknownst to many of us, mushrooms are not vegetables but fungi that often taste like beef (the Japanese call this taste component umami). Shiitake mushrooms are particularly meaty, with their dark-brown caps and bosky flavor. With a loaf of bread, this is almost a meal in itself.

**1 pound large shiitake mushrooms, wiped
clean, stems removed**

**3 tablespoons Garlic Oil (page 52), plus addi-
tional for drizzling**

⅓ cup dry white wine

Preheat the oven to 325°.

Line a baking sheet with a sheet of aluminum foil large enough to hold the mushrooms in a single layer. Sprinkle the baking sheet with the garlic oil and wine. Place the mushrooms stem side up on the baking sheet and sprinkle with coarse salt and freshly ground pepper. Bake 20 minutes. Turn the mushrooms over and bake 10 minutes longer. Remove from the oven.

Slice the mushrooms thickly and serve with pan juices. Drizzle with additional garlic oil.

Serves 5 or 6

Seared Sea Scallops
on Sweet Pea Puree

This lovely combination of sweet-fleshed scallops and sweet green peas is a perfect way to bring springtime into a meal in any season. Frozen petits pois, always available, produce the best results.

1 pound medium sea scallops (about 20)

1 (10-ounce) package frozen petits pois, defrosted

3½ tablespoons unsalted butter

Pat the scallops dry with paper towels and reserve.

Put the peas in a small pot with just enough water to cover. Add ½ teaspoon coarse salt. Cook briefly over medium-high heat until the peas are tender but still bright green, about 2 minutes.

Drain the peas, saving 6 tablespoons cooking water and reserving ¼ cup peas for garnish. Put the peas in a blender and puree at highest speed. Add 2 tablespoons of the butter, cut into small pieces, and 5 to 6 tablespoons cooking water, so that you have a very smooth but thick puree. You will have about 1¼ cups puree. Keep warm.

In a large nonstick skillet, melt ½ tablespoon of the remaining butter. Add the scallops and cook over high heat on both sides until golden.

In the center of large plates, spread ⅓ cup pea puree into a 5-inch-diameter circle. Place the reserved peas, like pearls, around each circle. Remove the scallops from the pan with a slotted spoon. Arrange 5 scallops per dish on top of the pea puree.

ADD-ONS

Add 2 tablespoons dry vermouth to scallop pan juices.

GRAPENOTES

An oh-so-elegant marriage with a bottle of chilled Meursault or a more unusual riesling Kabinett from a good German producer.

Add 4 tablespoons reserved water to pan juices. Whisk in the remaining 1 tablespoon butter and remove from the heat; the sauce will thicken. Add salt to taste and pour the juices around the pea puree. Serve immediately.

Serves 4

Smoked Salmon "Pitza"

Store-bought pita becomes an edible bed for flavored cream cheese and warm smoked salmon. Great for brunch—or for dinner in your silk pajamas. Just open a bottle of pink champagne! This dish is particularly memorable when made with "pastrami-cured salmon," a product occasionally available in specialty-food shops.

4 pita breads

4 ounces herbed goat cheese or scallion cream cheese

12 ounces thinly sliced smoked salmon or pastrami-cured salmon (see Note)

Preheat the oven to 425°.

Lay the pita breads flat on a large baking sheet. Whip the goat cheese until light and fluffy and spread the cheese evenly on the pita breads, leaving a border of ½ inch. Place the smoked salmon evenly on top to completely cover the cheese.

Bake 6 or 7 minutes, until salmon is warmed.

Serve on individual plates. If desired, cut each into 6 wedges, using a pizza cutter or very sharp knife.

Serves 4

Note: You can buy pastrami-cured salmon at many specialty-food stores (see Sources, page 291). It is cured and smoked with spices typically used for pastrami: coriander seed, bay leaves, garlic.

ADD-ONS

Sprinkle with tiny nonpareil capers and finely diced red onion.

GRAPENOTES

Try a bottle of a pink champagne like Iron Horse Brut Rosé or Mirabelle Rosé Brut. If you want to spend less and still have a good time, try Sakonnet Eye of the Storm blush wine from Rhode Island.

Tomato, Mozzarella, and Basil:
Six Styles

ADD-ONS

Serve any of these above with extra-virgin olive oil.

2 to 3 pounds very large ripe tomatoes (6),
depending on recipe

1 to 1½ pounds freshly made mozzarella
cheese, depending on recipe

1 large bunch fresh basil

TOMATO PUREE

Peel 1 or 2 ripe tomatoes, cut in half and squeeze out seeds. Put in a blender and frappé with a pinch of sea salt until smooth and frothy.

BASIL PUREE

Place ½ cup washed, dried, and tightly packed basil leaves in a blender. Add 2 to 3 tablespoons cold water and puree until very smooth. Add sea salt to taste and blend until incorporated.

I Mozzarella with Julienned Tomato and Basil

Cut *1 pound fresh mozzarella* into 6 thick slices, and spread them on a plate in a single layer or slightly overlapping. Cut the outer flesh off *3 large tomatoes*, reserving pulp, and cut into thin strips. Put in a bowl. Julienne as many fresh basil leaves as needed to equal the volume of the tomato strips. Add to the bowl and toss together with a pinch of sea salt. Place a mound of the julienned mixture on top of the cheese. Drizzle with 1½ tablespoons basil puree. Finely chop the reserved tomato pulp and use as a garnish surrounding the cheese.

II *Tomato, Basil, and Mozzarella Flower*

Cut a large, thick slice of tomato from the center of *6 tomatoes* with stems. Put the slices in a blender and puree with a pinch of sea salt. Cut *1 pound fresh mozzarella* into 6 thick slices. Using the remaining tomato parts, make "sandwiches" with mozzarella and fresh basil leaves as filling. Sprinkle with sea salt and freshly ground black pepper. Place on a pool of tomato puree.

III *Baked Tomato, Mozzarella, and Basil*

Preheat the oven to 400°. Cut ½ inch off the tops of *4 tomatoes*. Save for another use. Scoop out the tomato pulp and save for another use. Place 2 large basil leaves in the bottom of each tomato shell. Cut *½ pound fresh mozzarella* into 4 pieces. Fill each shell with cheese. Bake for 8 to 10 minutes, until the cheese melts. Garnish with fresh basil leaves. Optional: Serve warm with tomato or basil puree.

IV *Mozzarella and Tomato Skewers*

Place *4 tomatoes* stem side down. Make 4 equidistant slits almost to the bottom of each tomato, about ½ inch apart. Cut *1½ pounds fresh mozzarella* into 16 slices. Slip a piece of cheese into each slit, trimming excess cheese away with small sharp knife. Place two long wooden or decorative metal skewers lengthwise into each tomato. Cut between skewers. You will have 8 skewers. Sprinkle with sea salt and butcher-grind black pepper. Serve on a bed of fresh basil leaves.

V *Tomato and Mozzarella Pinwheels*

Cut 3 tomatoes into 9 thick slices (discard the tops and bottoms). Cut the slices in half to produce 18 half circles. Cut *1¼ pounds fresh mozzarella* into 9 slices and cut into half circles. Alternate cheese and tomatoes on plates in pinwheel fashion. Place basil leaves in center. Decorate the edges of the plates with teaspoonfuls of basil puree.

VI *Tomato and Mozzarella "Club"*

Cut ½ inch off the tops and bottoms of *6 tomatoes* and discard. Cut the tomatoes in half horizontally. Cut *1 pound fresh mozzarella* into 6 thick slices. Sandwich cheese and fresh basil leaves between thick tomato slices, trimming off excess cheese to make the cheese conform to the tomatoes' shapes. Place 4 toothpicks in each "sandwich," cut in quarters vertically, and turn quarters with points facing out. Serve with tomato puree, if desired.

I, II, V, and VI: Serves 6
III and IV: Serves 4

Salad Frisée with Lardons and Hot Vinegar Dressing

In abundantly stocked produce markets, you often find wispy heads of jade-green frisée from France. Heartier domestic chicory makes a more assertive substitute. This is a warming first course that can easily become a main course with the addition of whole-wheat croutons and Roquefort cheese.

ADD-ONS

Delicious with crumbled blue cheese on top of the salad.

2 large heads frisée lettuce or 1 large head chickory

8 ounces pancetta, in ¼-inch slices

¼ cup good-quality red wine vinegar, or Herbes de Provence Vinegar (page 69)

Wash the lettuce and dry well in a salad spinner. Tear the leaves coarsely. Reserve.

Cut pancetta slices into ¼-inch-wide strips, or lardons. Cook over medium heat in a nonstick skillet until the fat is rendered and the pancetta is beginning to crisp. Remove the pancetta with a slotted spoon; reserve the rendered fat in the skillet.

Divide the lettuce evenly onto 4 to 6 plates. Divide the pancetta evenly over the lettuce.

Add the vinegar carefully to the hot fat in the pan. Cook over high heat for 1 minute, adding a pinch of salt. Pour the hot dressing over the lettuce. Serve immediately and add pepper to taste.

Serves 4 to 6

Chapter 8

Soups and Pasta

Soups and pasta, often designated for the beginning of a meal, are also meals in themselves. Sometimes soup and pasta even coexist in a single dish, as in Fennel, Leek, and Orzo Soup, or Ginger Pepperpot, "Glass" Noodles.

In the Italian culture, pasta is an individual course—a bridge between the antipasto and the main course. Rarely does it take center stage. But here in America, where the structure of one's repast is as individual as one's mode of dress, pasta is "as you like it!"

Carrot-Ginger Velvet

The development of a recipe: Sounded delicious in my head, could almost taste it on my palate, could see its brilliant color and feel its creamy texture—like velvet on my tongue. But it took many tries to get it right.

GRAPENOTE

An off-dry domestic gewürztraminer from Chateau Ste. Michelle in Washington State would be a lovely choice.

> 1½ pounds fresh carrots (with carrot tops, if possible), plus 2 large carrots for roasting (see Note)
>
> 3-inch piece of fresh ginger, yielding 1½ teaspoons fresh ginger juice (see Note)
>
> ½ cup heavy cream

Trim the carrots, saving the carrot tops. Peel the carrots and cut them into 1-inch pieces. Put them in a medium-size pot with 4 cups water and 1½ teaspoons salt. Bring to a boil, lower the heat, and cook, covered, for 35 minutes, or until the carrots are very soft.

Transfer the carrots to a food processor and puree until very smooth, slowly adding cooking water as you go. All the water should be incorporated. Add the ginger juice and heavy cream and process.

Gently heat the soup before serving, adding a few tablespoons of water if necessary.

Serve with julienned oven-roasted carrots and a few leaves from the carrot tops.

Makes 1 quart, serving 4 or 5

Notes: To oven-roast carrots: Preheat the oven to 400°. Put the washed, unpeeled carrots in a pie tin or on roasting pan and bake 50 minutes, or until soft. Let cool. Peel. Cut into matchstick-size julienne.

To prepare ginger juice: Peel the ginger with a small, sharp knife. Grate on the large holes of a box grater. Put the grated ginger in paper towel and squeeze the juice from ginger. You will have about 1½ to 2 teaspoons.

Port Consommé

You expect consommé to start a meal, but this fine soup also is a sophisticated "intermezzo" to cleanse the palate between courses. It is so interesting in flavor, it could even "consummate" a meal, after the cheese course but before the cigars.

¾ cup tawny port wine

1 cinnamon stick

3 cups beef broth

Put the port, the cinnamon stick, and 1/4 teaspoon whole black peppercorns in a small, heavy enamel pot. Reduce over low heat to ½ cup.

Meanwhile, in another pot, reduce the beef broth slowly until it becomes 2½ cups.

Pour the reduced port through a strainer and add it to the reduced beef broth. Heat gently before serving.

Serves 6

Serve with a thin lemon slice floating on top.

"Cream" of Spinach Soup

In the Italian kitchen, the word crema when used for soups refers to a smooth, thick texture, not necessarily to the addition of cream. There's no cream here either, but lots of fresh spinach and potatoes bound with butter. This is comfort food at its most brilliant—in color, that is.

ADD-ONS

Shave Parmigiano-
Reggiano on top, or
dust lightly with
freshly grated nutmeg.

1 pound boiling potatoes, peeled

1 pound fresh spinach leaves, stems removed

5 tablespoons unsalted butter

In a large, heavy pot, bring 8 cups of water to a boil with 1 teaspoon salt. Halve the potatoes lengthwise and cut halves into ½-inch-thick slices. Put the slices in the pot and cook over medium-high heat for 20 minutes.

Add the spinach and cook 10 minutes longer. Do not overcook, or the spinach will lose its bright-green color.

Transfer the spinach and potatoes to a food processor with a slotted spoon, reserving 2½ cups cooking liquid. Process until very smooth, adding the butter 1 tablespoon at a time.

Put the spinach puree back in the pot and slowly add the cooking liquid until you reach the desired consistency. Reheat gently and add salt and pepper to taste. Serve hot.

Makes 8 cups, serving 8 to 10

Fournade: Creamy Chickpea Soup

This unusual soup is a specialty of southern France (and Liguria, where it is known as panizza*), but a touch of aromatic Egyptian spices, called* dukkah*, makes it quite global. Add a few drops of truffle oil and this humble "soupe au bâton" (literally "stirred with a stick") is deserving of a silver spoon.*

> 1 cup chickpea flour
>
> 4 cups chicken or vegetable broth, preferably
>   homemade
>
> 4 tablespoons extra-virgin olive oil

Combine the chickpea flour and broth in the bowl of an electric mixer and beat until smooth. Pour into a large heavy pot and add 2 tablespoons of the olive oil, 1 teaspoon salt, and $\frac{1}{8}$ teaspoon each finely ground white and black pepper.

Bring to a boil, then immediately lower the heat and simmer 10 minutes, stirring often with a wooden spoon or wire whisk. The soup will thicken quickly. Add water to thin as desired. Drizzle with the remaining 2 tablespoons of oil.

Makes about 4 cups, serving 6

ADD-ONS

Sprinkle with some Egyptian Spices, or a few drops of truffle oil.

Egyptian Spices:
2 tablespoons sesame seeds

1 tablespoon coriander seeds

2 teaspoons cumin seeds

Put the spices in a nonstick skillet and cook a few minutes over low heat until fragrant. Grind to a fine powder in a spice grinder. Put in a small bowl and add a liberal pinch of salt.

Soupy Red Beans with Smoked Ham

Make enough to last a week, because the simple flavors deepen day by day. A flourish of sweet-and-sour greens will make your mouth water. Follow with Spoonbread Custard (page 188).

1 pound dried red kidney beans

2 medium onions, peeled and quartered

1 smoked ham hock, split, or 8 ounces smoked pork butt

Pick over the beans and wash them. Soak them overnight in cold water to cover by 2 inches.

Drain the beans. Put them in a pot with fresh water to cover by 2 inches. Add the onions and ham hock. Bring to a boil, lower the heat, and cover, and simmer the beans 1 hour, periodically skimming off the foam that rises to the surface. Add 2 teaspoons salt and cook 1½ hours longer over low heat, uncovered. Stir often. The beans will be very tender and the soup will thicken.

Add freshly ground black pepper to taste. Cut off any meat from the bones, dice it, and add it to the beans. Serve hot.

Makes 7½ to 8 cups, serving 6 to 8

ADD-ONS

Serve with Pickled Greens (page 91). Add a few bay leaves and 2 peeled cloves of garlic to the pot when cooking. To make this soup a main course, serve over fluffy long-grain rice.

GRAPENOTE

Served with a glass of spicy cold gewürztraminer, this is an interesting way to begin a dinner. As a meal in itself, try it with a good Belgian beer.

Pickled Greens

An unusual preparation of bitter greens that winds up sweet and sassy. Use as a cool topping for Soupy Red Beans (page 90), or alongside some Barbecued Pork Pull (page 158). Bring on the biscuits!

> 1 pound mustard greens, collard greens, or kale
> ¾ cup sugar
> ½ cup vinegar

Wash, dry, and coarsely chop the greens, including stems. In a large pot, combine 2 cups water, the sugar, the vinegar, 1½ tablespoons kosher salt, and 1 teaspoon whole black peppercorns. Bring to a boil, lower the heat, and cook 5 minutes.

Add the greens to the pot. Cook 2 minutes. Let cool. Pack in a 1-quart jar with lid. Cover and let sit 2 days, refrigerated, before using.

Makes 1 quart

Avocado Velouté, Fino Sherry

This is a chilled soup with a haunting aftertaste. It is three-ingredient alchemy, because this dish tastes nothing like its components. No one will guess what it is, but everyone will ask for more.

ADD-ONS

Garnish with a dollop of crème fraîche or chopped smoked almonds.

GRAPENOTE

Serve with small glass of fino sherry.

> 1 large ripe avocado
>
> 1½ cups homemade chicken broth (page 96) or canned
>
> 1 tablespoon fino sherry

Remove the pit from the avocado and then peel the avocado with a sharp knife. Cut into ½-inch pieces. Put the chicken broth and 1 cup water in a medium-size heavy saucepan and bring to a boil. Lower the heat and add the avocado. Simmer 2 minutes.

Transfer the contents of the saucepan to a blender. Process until the soup is very smooth and creamy. Stir in the sherry and chill well.

Makes 3½ cups

Fennel, Leek, and Orzo Soup

The most Italian of vegetables, fennel has marvelous digestive properties—which is a good thing, because this soup thickens like porridge. It is an Italian custom to put the sweet and versatile finocchio on the table, like a fruit, at the end of a meal.

> 4 cups finely diced fennel (1 large bulb, about 1½ pounds)
>
> 1 large bunch leeks (3 large leeks), enough to make 4 cups finely diced
>
> 1 cup uncooked orzo

Cut off the fennel fronds from the fennel bulb and reserve for a garnish. Remove any brown spots from the fennel bulb.

Clean the leeks thoroughly and dice finely—you should have 4 cups.

Put 8 cups water in a large, heavy pot and bring to a boil. Add the fennel and orzo and 1½ teaspoons salt. Lower the heat, cover, and simmer 50 minutes.

With a large ladle, remove 4 cups of soup from the pot and puree until smooth in a food processor. Return the soup to the pot and continue to cook, uncovered, over medium heat for 8 to 10 minutes. Add salt and freshly ground black pepper to taste. Chop the fennel fronds and use them to garnish the soup.

Makes 11 cups, serving 10

ADD-ONS

Drizzle with extra-virgin olive oil or freshly grated Parmesan cheese. The next day, when the soup is very thick, serve with a poached egg on top.

Curried Lentil Soup

ADD-ONS

Add a splash of Madeira to the hot soup before serving.

This could be my soupe du jour 365 days a year. A soupçon of Madeira makes a big splash by transforming this legume into something lusty and aromatic. But it's great even without it.

⅔ cup French green lentils (see Note)

½ cup finely chopped shallots

2 teaspoons good-quality curry powder

Put the lentils, the shallots, the curry powder, 4 cups of water, and 2 teaspoons salt in a medium-size heavy saucepan and bring to a boil. Lower heat, cover, and simmer 25 minutes, or until tender.

Process in a food processor until smooth. The soup will still have a rough texture because of the lentils. You could pass it through a sieve, but I find the roughness appealing.

Makes 2 cups, serving 2

Note: French green lentils are found at specialty-food stores (see Sources, page 289).

"Fire and Ice" Gazpacho

Add as much fire as you desire. Flash-chill in the freezer just until ice crystals begin to appear, then serve. Add a splash of pepper vodka just for fun.

2 cups Pomi brand strained tomatoes

1½ tablespoons hot sauce (see Note)

2 large red bell peppers (¾ pound)

Put the strained tomatoes and hot sauce in a medium-size bowl.

Core and seed the peppers and process in a food processor until pureed.

Add the pepper puree to the tomatoes. Mix well and transfer to a medium-size heavy enamel pot. Simmer 10 minutes and add freshly ground black pepper to taste.

Let cool, then chill in the refrigerator until very cold.

Serves 3 or 4

ADD-ONS

Add chopped cooked shrimp, diced avocado, sour cream, cilantro leaves, or chopped cucumber as a garnish.

GRAPENOTE

Serve a short glass of iced pepper vodka on the side. Or keep the "fire" low and go for a fino. If you add lots of "fire" to the dish, go with a very "hoppy" beer.

Note: Use a hot sauce such as Frank's or Durkee's, not Tabasco, which is much more concentrated.

Chicken Broth 1-2-3

I'm a morning kind of person and love to start cooking early in the day, especially on the weekends, when I generally make soups and stocks. Even if you've never made stock before, here's a satisfying way to start.

This stock is easy, but give it time to simmer gently. "The pot should only smile with heat" (French proverb). Once the soup is strained, you can reduce it further until it becomes thick and syrupy, for what professionals call glace de volaille.

5 pounds chicken necks and backs

12 ounces carrots, with carrot tops

4 large yellow onions

Wash the chicken pieces and pat dry with paper towels. Peel the carrots and cut them into 1-inch pieces. Wash the carrot tops and chop enough for ½ cup. Peel the onions and cut into thin wedges.

Put all ingredients in a large heavy pot with 5 to 6 quarts cold water to cover and 1 teaspoon whole black peppercorns. Bring just to a boil, lower the heat, and simmer 2½ hours, skimming off any foam that forms on the surface.

Line a strainer with cheesecloth and pour the broth through into a large bowl. At this point you can put the strained broth in a large clean pot and reduce to desired consistency.

Let the broth cool and refrigerate it until ready to use, removing any fat. If serving as soup, return the strained broth to the pot, add the cooked onions and carrots, heat, and serve. The broth or soup can be kept for up to two days. Before using broth, skim the fat, then bring to a boil and boil for 5 minutes to eliminate any bacteria. Makes about 4 quarts. If reducing to use as a stock, reduce to 3 quarts.

Makes 4 quarts broth or 3 quarts stock

ADD-ONS

You can add celery or parsnips if you please. As a treat, I put the chicken fat skimmed from the stock in a small ramekin, chill it, and serve it instead of butter with bakery rye bread.

"Sopa de Salsa"

Totally fun. Serve in large colorful mugs with a basket of warm taco chips. Control the heat with your choice of salsa, from mild to incendiary. Serve with beer and you've got a great little meal.

> 3½ cups half-and-half
>
> 1 medium onion, finely chopped (¾ cup)
>
> 1 (12-ounce) jar medium-hot salsa

Bring the half-and-half and onions to a boil in a medium-size pot. Lower the heat and simmer for 15 minutes. Add the salsa, and simmer 5 minutes. Puree in a blender.

Pour the soup back into the pot and simmer 5 minutes or until hot, letting the flavors mingle.

Makes 4¾ cups, serving 4 or 5

ADD-ONS

Garnish with a dollop of sour cream or Crisp Tortilla Ribbons (page 98).

Crisp Tortilla Ribbons

2 corn tortillas
2 tablespoons vegetable oil

Cut the tortillas into $\frac{1}{16}$-inch-wide ribbons. In a small nonstick skillet, heat the oil and fry the ribbons until crisp. Drain and sprinkle lightly with salt. Set aside until ready to use.

Makes 4 to 5 portions

Yellow Turnip Soubise

In the classic French repertoire, a soubise sauce is made from onions and thickened with rice. This soup incorporates onions and rice plus the pleasing, burnished flavor of slow-roasted rutabagas, also known as Swedes or Swedish turnips.

> **2 pounds yellow turnips, peeled and trimmed, cut into large chunks**
>
> **1 pound onions, peeled and cut into large chunks**
>
> **6 tablespoons long-grain rice**

Put the turnips, the onions, 6 cups water, and 2 teaspoons salt in a large heavy pot and bring to a boil. Add the rice, mix well, and cover. Lower heat and simmer 50 minutes, or until vegetables are very soft.

In several batches, puree contents of pot in a food processor until very, very smooth. Return the puree to the pot. Adjust the seasoning with salt and freshly ground black pepper.

Reheat before serving. This soup gets better as it sits and is decidedly better the next day.

Makes 9 1/2 cups, serving 9 to 10

ADD-ONS

Garnish with coarsely chopped fresh tarragon leaves. Pass a small pitcher of heavy cream for those who will.

GRAPENOTE

Its sweet, earthy essence makes this soup a good match with a California viognier, a white Côtes du Rhône, or a white Rioja.

Beer and Stilton Soup

ADD-ONS

If you want a thicker soup, dissolve 1 tablespoon arrowroot in 1 tablespoon cold water. Whisk into the hot soup and cook until soup thickens. Garnish with fresh chervil. Serve with homemade Beer Bread (opposite) or caraway rye.

GRAPENOTES

A real "taste match" with Alsatian riesling from Trimbach, or an ice-cold beer of your choice.

Don't expect a bowl of something thick and creamy, because this unusual preparation is a heady consommé worthy of sophisticated guests. Use amber beer from a local microbrewery—and during the holidays try a sweeter Christmas beer. Very après-ski.

6 cups homemade chicken broth (page 96) or canned

1½ cups amber beer

12 ounces good-quality English Stilton cheese

In a medium-size heavy pot, bring chicken stock and beer to a rapid boil. Lower the heat and cook over medium heat for 20 minutes, or until liquid is reduced to 5 cups.

Crumble the Stilton into small pieces and add it to the simmering broth, slowly stirring with a wooden spoon. Add freshly ground pepper to taste. Continue to cook for 5 to 10 minutes, until slightly thickened.

Makes 5½ cups, serving 5 or 6

Beer Bread

6 tablespoons sugar
12 ounces beer, at room temperature
3 cups self-rising flour

Preheat the oven to 350°.

Place the sugar in a medium-size enamel pot and cook over medium heat until it is caramelized. Remove from the heat when the sugar is a light-brown liquid.

Pour in the beer slowly. The liquid will foam and bubble. Mix well with a wooden spoon until all the sugar is dissolved.

Put the flour in the bowl of an electric mixer. Add a pinch of salt and slowly pour in the liquid. Mix until the ingredients are incorporated and the dough is smooth.

Place the dough in a 9-inch nonstick loaf pan. Bake 55 to 60 minutes; the bread is done when a toothpick comes out clean. Remove bread from the oven and let cool on a rack.

Makes one loaf

Red Wine Onion Soup

It has been said that the only good onion soup is a simple one. And it doesn't get more simple than this! Substitute beef broth for wine for a more classic rendition. Make sure the onions are thoroughly caramelized (dark brown and soft), for the deepest, sweetest flavor.

3½ tablespoons unsalted butter

2 pounds spanish onions, peeled, halved, and thinly sliced

1 cup cabernet sauvignon or other robust red wine

Melt the butter in large heavy pot with a cover. Add the onions and sauté over medium heat for 30 to 40 minutes, until onions are soft and caramelized (they will be a deep-brown color). Stir often, scraping up the browned bits with a wooden spoon.

Add the wine and cook, stirring frequently, until most of the liquid has evaporated.

Add 6 cups water, 2 teaspoons salt, and freshly ground white pepper to taste. Bring to a boil. Lower the heat, cover, and simmer 20 minutes. Puree 2 cups of soup (with onions) in a food processor until smooth.

Add this mixture to the soup pot and cook 10 minutes longer, uncovered. Serve very hot.

Makes 6½ cups, serving 4 to 6

ADD-ONS

Serve the soup with grated Asiago cheese, or put a toasted crouton on the top of each bowl of soup and cover with a thin slice of fontina or Gruyère cheese. Put under the broiler until the cheese begins to melt and brown lightly.

GRAPENOTE

Often a fruity Beaujolais is a good companion to classic onion soup, but this soup should be served with the same full-bodied cabernet used in the dish.

An Unusual Borscht: Roasted Beet, Squash, and Yogurt

There are as many borschts as there are former members of the Soviet Union, but the unifying ingredient is generally the scarlet beet. This recipe gains its intense flavor from roasting the vegetables before pureeing them.

1½ pounds large beets with beet green tops

2 pounds Hubbard or butternut squash

1 cup plain yogurt

Preheat the oven to 400°.

Wash the beets. Remove the green tops and reserve. Cut the beets in half. Cut the squash in quarters and remove the seeds. Place the beets and squash cut side down in a baking pan. Sprinkle with ¼ cup water. Roast for 1½ hours, or until soft. (Turn the vegetables over halfway through cooking, adding more water if necessary.)

Remove from the oven and let cool 10 minutes. Remove the squash pulp from the skin and puree it in a food processor. Peel the beets, cut them into small pieces, and add them to the processor. Puree until smooth. Add the yogurt and puree again. Add ⅓ to ½ cup cold water and 1 teaspoon salt. Process until smooth and creamy. Serve hot or cold.

Garnish with additional yogurt, or with beet greens that have been steamed and chopped.

Makes 4½ cups, serving 4 to 5

ADD-ONS

If not using beet greens, garnish with finely chopped onions or scallions, or chopped cucumber. Serve with Caraway Cheese Crisps (see page 104).

Caraway Cheese Crisps

1 medium-size loaf unsliced rye bread with caraway seeds
6 tablespoons unsalted butter
⅔ cup grated Parmesan cheese

Preheat the oven to 275°. With a sharp knife, slice the bread paper-thin. Melt the butter in the saucepan and add the cheese. Spread the mixture on one side of each slice of bread. Place the bread on an ungreased baking sheet and bake for 20 to 25 minutes, until the edges start to curl and the bread is crisp. Stores well.

Makes 30 crisps

Chilled Cauliflower Crème

Here's an elegant way to serve this aggressive relative of the cabbage. But don't keep it more than a day or two, because its cabbagey essense will surely grow.

1 large head cauliflower

1 bunch scallions (5–6)

½ cup half-and-half

Trim the cauliflower of its green leaves. Separate the cauliflower into florets and chop the core into pieces. In a large pot, put all the cauliflower, 3½ cups water, and 1¾ teaspoons salt.

Trim the scallions. Remove the dark-green tops and save. Cut the remaining white and light-green parts into 1-inch lengths and add them to the pot.

Bring to a boil. Lower the heat, cover, and cook 20 to 25 minutes, until very soft. Transfer the contents of the pot to the bowl of a food processor and puree until very smooth. You may need to do this in two batches. Add half-and-half and freshly ground white pepper. Refrigerate until very cold.

Garnish with scallion tops that have been finely chopped.

Makes 5½ cups, serving 5 to 6

ADD-ONS

Delicious served in small chilled cups with a teaspoon of black caviar on top.

GRAPENOTE

If serving with caviar, celebrate with a fairly yeasty sparkler with some bottle age: Schramsberg blanc de noirs or Charles Heidsieck.

Brie and Pear Soup

ADD-ONS

Garnish with whole pink peppercorns or lightly toasted sliced almonds.

GRAPENOTE

Nice with a glass of bold, floral chardonnay like Au Bon Climat from Santa Barbara.

According to Ralph Waldo Emerson, "there are only ten minutes in the life of a pear when it is perfect to eat." Luckily, this soup is perfect anytime. Use Bartlett pears in the early fall, ripe Comice in the winter, fragrant Bosc and Anjou when available. Make sure the Brie is also ripe —preferably a double-crème *from France.*

2 large ripe pears (about 1 pound)

2 cups homemade chicken broth (page 96) or canned

8 ounces double-cream Brie cheese

Peel the pears. Cut them into thick slices, removing the seeds. Put the chicken broth and pears in a large pot and simmer 10 to 15 minutes, until the pears are very soft.

Transfer the pears and broth to a food processor and process until very smooth. Return to the pot and simmer.

Trim the rind from the brie and cut the cheese into small pieces. Slowly add the cheese and stir with a wooden spoon until melted. The soup should be creamy and smooth.

Serves 4 or 5

Ginger Pepperpot, "Glass" Noodles

Ginger juice is easily extracted: Grate a knobby chunk of peeled fresh ginger on a box grater; wrap the shavings in a paper towel and gently squeeze.

Cellophane noodles made from bean curd look like strings of glass. You can use soba noodles or angel hair pasta as a substitute.

6 cups homemade chicken broth (page 96) or canned

4-ounce piece fresh ginger

4 ounces cellophane noodles

In a large heavy pot, toast ½ teaspoon white peppercorns until fragrant. Add the chicken broth and bring to a boil. Lower the heat and simmer 20 minutes, or until the broth is reduced to 4½ cups.

Meanwhile, peel the ginger. Cut off a 1-inch piece and mince; you will have about 1 tablespoon. Set aside in a small bowl. Grate the rest of the ginger on the large holes of box grater. Put the grated ginger in a paper towel and squeeze the juice into another small bowl. You should have about 4½ teaspoons juice. Add to the minced ginger.

When the broth has reduced, add the ginger juice, minced ginger, and cellophane noodles. Cook 5 minutes, or until noodles are soft.

Serves 4

Garnish with finely chopped scallions and/or fresh cilantro leaves. The soup can also be served with strips of cooked chicken or roast pork.

Sauerkraut "Hangover" Soup

This is the best way I know to cure a hangover and have a comforting meal at the same time (but then again, I'm of Hungarian descent). Serve with little sandwiches of buttered black bread.

1 pound sauerkraut in plastic bag

3½ tablespoons packed dark brown sugar

1 (28-ounce) can crushed tomatoes in puree

Put sauerkraut with its liquid and 3 tablespoons of the brown sugar in a large enamel pot and cook over medium heat for 5 minutes.

Add the crushed tomatoes and puree. Add 2 cups water, 1 teaspoon kosher salt, and freshly ground white and black pepper. Cover and simmer 30 minutes. Add remaining ½ tablespoon brown sugar, to balance flavors. Cook 1 to 2 minutes uncovered. Serve hot.

Makes 7 cups, serving 7 to 8

ADD-ONS

Sprinkle the soup with caraway seeds. Or put the soup in onion-soup crocks, place a slice of muenster cheese on top, and broil for 30 seconds, or until cheese melts and begins to brown.

GRAPENOTE

If you don't have a hangover, try a good dark beer named Samuel . . . Adams or Smith.

Yellow Pea and Bacon Potage

The humorist Bennett Cerf described good manners as "the noise you don't make when you're eating soup." So put manners aside and enjoy. This is one of my favorites.

> **8 ounces dried yellow split peas**
>
> **2 ounces medium-size onions**
>
> **4 slices bacon, cut into ½-inch pieces**

Soak the yellow peas overnight.

The next day, peel the onions and cut them into 8 wedges.

Put the bacon in a medium-size heavy pot and cook 1 to 2 minutes, until the fat begins to melt. Add the onions and sauté the bacon and onions over medium heat for 10 minutes, or until they begin to brown lightly.

Add the drained yellow peas and 3 cups of fresh water. Bring to a boil, lower the heat, and cook, covered, for 45 minutes, stirring often.

Puree 1 cup of the soup in a blender and add it back to the soup pot with ½ teaspoon salt. Cook 5 or 6 minutes, adding more water if soup is too thick.

Makes 4½ cups, serving 4 or 5

ADD-ONS

Sprinkle with a little finely snipped fresh sage.

GRAPENOTE

This soup is a good candidate for an Alsatian pinot blanc from Leon Mader; a good imported Pilsner would also be appropriate.

Veal Tortellini,
Turkish Yogurt Sauce

ADD-ONS

Add ½ teaspoon
sweet paprika to the
melted butter. This
dish also works with
tortellini filled with
spinach.

GRAPENOTE

Delicious paired with
your favorite flavor-
packed sauvignon
blanc.

*Gail, my globe-trotting sister-in-law, lived in Istanbul for five years. In
addition to being fluent in Turkish (and Japanese), she is a fabulous
cook and often uses this simple Turkish sauce as a topping for pasta. She
makes her own tortellini—but you can buy yours.*

> **1 pound veal tortellini**
>
> **1 cup Labaneh (opposite), at room
> temperature**
>
> **2 tablespoons unsalted butter**

Boil the tortellini in salted water—they will rise to the top of the pot
when done. While the pasta is cooking, beat the labaneh with a whisk
until it loosens. Make sure it is at room temperature.

Drain the pasta well in a colander. Place it in a serving bowl and
top with the labaneh. Quickly melt the butter, being careful not to let
it brown, and pour it over the pasta. Pass the pepper mill.

Serves 4 to 5

Labaneh
(Yogurt Cheese)

2 cups nonfat plain yogurt
½ clove garlic (optional)

Line a strainer with two layers of cheesecloth. Place the yogurt in the strainer. Place the strainer over a bowl to catch the liquid. Let sit at room temperature 8 hours, or until very thick.

If using garlic, push it through a garlic press and add it to the labaneh. Stir well and refrigerate.

Makes 1 cup

Garlic and Oil Spaghetti

My best friend, Arthur Schwartz, food critic of New York's Daily News *and host of the popular radio show* FoodTalk, *says, "Fifty million Italians can't be wrong! Spaghetti 'aglio e olio' is like mother's milk in the land of macaroni."*

4 medium cloves garlic

6 tablespoons fruity olive oil

8 ounces spaghetti

Bring a large pot of salted water to a boil.

Peel the garlic and finely chop. In a small skillet, combine the garlic and olive oil and cook the garlic over low heat until it is pale brown. Do not let it get darker or it will be bitter.

Drain the spaghetti when done ("al dente" for many brands takes 12 minutes), saving ⅓ cup of the cooking water.

Put the ⅓ cup cooking water, the garlic, the oil, and the well-drained pasta in a large, heated serving bowl. Toss gently and season to taste with salt and pepper.

Serves 3 or 4

ADD-ONS

Add 1½ teaspoons red pepper flakes when browning the garlic.

GRAPENOTE

Arthur says to serve an unpretentious, simple red wine from Italy. And yes, you *can* still get Chianti in a straw basket, or *fiasco!*

Linguine Riviera, Red Sardine Sauce

This dish conjures up memories of outdoor dining on the Riviera: blue skies, cypress trees, and a calming azure sea. Follow with a steamy bowl of fresh-cooked mussels and crusty garlic bread.

2 cups crushed tomatoes in puree

1 cup sardines in olive oil (skinless and boneless)

8 ounces linguine pasta

In a large nonstick skillet, heat the crushed tomatoes and puree. Add the sardines and their oil and cook over low heat 5 or 6 minutes, breaking up the sardines with a wooden spoon.

Bring a large pot of salted water to a boil. Add the pasta and cook until al dente.

Add ¼ cup pasta cooking water to the red sauce and a generous amount of freshly ground black pepper.

Drain the pasta well and serve with the hot tomato sauce on top. Makes 2 cups sauce.

Serves 3 to 4

ADD-ONS

Add a handful of freshly chopped Italian parsley.

GRAPENOTE

Try something ultra-rustic from southern Italy or Sicily, like Aglianico del Vulture or Terrale Rosso.

Cheese Raviolini, Roasted Pumpkin Sauce

Add-Ons

Thinly slice Pecorino Romano cheese (with peppercorns, if available) with a sharp cheese knife. Serve atop the steamy bowl of pasta and sauce.

Grapenote

Try a chardonnay with a touch of oak from California or Australia.

Pasta di zucca is a familiar dish in northern Italy. Here I use slow-roasted pumpkin as a delectable sauce for cheese-filled raviolini (little ravioli). Sprinkle with toasted pumpkin seeds for added crunch.

> **2 pounds fresh pumpkin or Hubbard squash**
>
> **2 cups homemade chicken broth (page 96) or canned**
>
> **1 pound cheese raviolini (see Note)**

Preheat the oven to 400°.

Cut the pumpkin into several large pieces, removing any seeds or membrane. Reserve seeds if using for garnish (see Note). Place pumpkin in a baking pan, flesh side down, and pour ¼ cup water over the top. Bake for 1 hour, turning over after 30 minutes. The pumpkin will be lightly caramelized.

Meanwhile, reduce the chicken broth until you have 1½ cups. Keep warm.

Remove the pumpkin from the oven. Scrape the flesh from the skin and put in a blender or a food processor. Blend until very smooth, slowly adding the reduced broth. Taste the sauce, adding salt if needed. Keep warm.

Cook the raviolini in boiling salted water until tender. Drain well. Serve with the hot pumpkin sauce. Add coarsely ground black pepper to taste, or scatter with toasted pumpkin seeds.

Serves 5 to 6

Notes: Cheese raviolini are available in the refrigerated section of many supermarkets.

To toast pumpkin seeds: Pour boiling water over seeds in a small bowl and steep for 30 minutes. Drain well and pat dry with a paper towel. Bake on a baking sheet in a 300° oven for 25 minutes, then sprinkle with salt.

Hungarian Cabbage and Noodles

This was my comfort food when I was growing up with my beautiful Hungarian mother. Recently, I prowled Budapest looking for a version better than hers, but I never found one. You can also sauté some onion with the cabbage, as she often does.

1 large head green cabbage

½ cup (1 stick) unsalted butter

12 ounces medium-wide egg noodles

With a sharp knife, shred the cabbage into ¼-inch-wide slices. Place in a large bowl and sprinkle with kosher salt. Cover with a plate to weight it down and refrigerate overnight. Put in a pan to collect any liquid. The next day, turn the cabbage out into a colander and squeeze dry.

In a large pan, melt the butter and add the cabbage. Sauté over medium heat until the cabbage is light brown and very soft, 30 to 40 minutes.

Cook the noodles according to the package directions. Drain the noodles and toss them with the cabbage, adding lots of freshly ground black pepper.

Serves 4

ADD-ONS

Slice 1 large onion very thin and sauté it with the cabbage. Sprinkle with caraway seeds.

GRAPENOTE

Serve with a chilled barrel-fermented sauvignon blanc from California, one from Duckhorn or Silverado. Or for a more sophisticated pairing, try a Hungarian Tokay with a degree of sweetness. Serve chilled.

Farfalle with Broccoli, Broccoli-Butter Sauce

ADD-ONS

Shower with julienned basil leaves.

GRAPENOTE

Try a dry chenin blanc from another country, such as New Zealand, Chile, or Argentina, or savor one of the semillon-chardonnay blends from Australia, like Wynns, or Trident, from Seaview Bay.

Although there are more than 600 shapes of pasta, some varieties have a special affinity for certain ingredients. Bowties and broccoli florets make a great-looking plate of food. Ingenuity turns the woody stems into a sublime sauce.

1 large head broccoli (1 pound)

8 ounces farfalle (bowtie) pasta

3 tablespoons butter, cold

Cut the broccoli buds into small florets, leaving only ½ inch of the stem. Reserve.

Peel the remaining stems and cut them into 1-inch pieces. Cook in 1¼ cups salted water for about 25 minutes, covered, in a small pot. When the stems are very soft, transfer the contents of the pot to a blender. Puree the stems and water until very smooth. Add the butter, cut in small pieces, and process. Add a little water if necessary to make a smooth sauce. Add salt and pepper to taste and transfer to a small pot.

Meanwhile, cook the pasta in a pot of salted boiling water for about 10 minutes. Add the broccoli florets to the pot and cook 3 to 4 minutes, until broccoli and pasta are tender.

Heat the sauce gently and pour over the drained pasta.

Serves 4 (1¼ to 1⅓ cups sauce)

Orecchiette with Endive and Sun-Dried Tomatoes

Sun-dried tomatoes marinated in olive oil should become a staple in your pantry. They add a sweet acidity to dishes, and a Mediterranean spin. Tossed with orecchiette pasta ("little ears") and long strips of "chlorophyll-challenged" endive, they make this a happening dish. Serve steaming on a big oval platter, sprinkled with tiny nonpareil capers for company.

8 ounces sun-dried tomatoes in oil

12 ounces endive (3 medium-to-large)

8 ounces orecchiette pasta

Drain the oil from the tomatoes and place the oil in a large skillet. Cut the tomatoes in half and add them to the oil. Slice the endive into ¼-inch-thick slices (hold the knife on the diagonal to make oval-shaped slices). Add to the oil. Cook over medium-high heat until the endive is soft and the tomatoes are tender, about 10 minutes. Add salt and freshly ground black pepper to taste.

Meanwhile, cook the pasta for 12 to 15 minutes in boiling salted water or until done. Drain well. Put the pasta on a warm platter and cover thoroughly with sauce. Serve hot, or cold as a salad.

Serves 4

ADD-ONS

Scatter 1 tablespoon small capers on top of the sauce.

GRAPENOTE

Stylish with white or rosé: Try a viognier from the Rhône, or Rouvière Rosé or Bandol Rosé from Provence.

Angel's Food
I and II

Cappellini, also known as angel's hair, are long superfine strands of pasta available both dried and fresh. I like to use fresh cappellini to toss with saline black caviar, and dried cappellini to bathe in truffle oil. This is truly the "food of the gods."

I *Angel Hair Pasta with Caviar*

12 ounces fresh angel hair pasta

6 tablespoons unsalted butter

½ cup sevruga or osetra caviar

Boil the pasta in a large pot of salted water. Cook until just tender but not soft. This should take only about 2 minutes. Drain in a colander.

Meanwhile, melt the butter gently, being careful not to let it brown.

Put the pasta in a large, warm bowl. Pour the hot melted butter over the pasta. Toss. Add the caviar and toss again. Serve immediately.

Serves 4 to 6

ADD-ONS

Add a few drops of fresh lemon juice or garnish with a long strip of lemon zest, gently twisted.

GRAPENOTE

Only a glass of weighty champagne will do. How about nonvintage Bollinger or, since you're splurging, Dom Pérignon or Krug?

II *Angel Hair Pasta with Truffle Oil*

> 8 ounces dried angel hair pasta
>
> 3 tablespoons truffle oil—plus additional for
>   drizzling if desired
>
> ½ cup grated Parmigiano-Reggiano

Bring a large pot of salted water to a boil. Add the pasta and cook until tender, about 8 minutes, being careful not to overcook. Drain the pasta in a colander, saving ¼ cup of the cooking water. Put the pasta in a warmed ceramic bowl.

Add the truffle oil, a little cooking water, salt to taste, and a generous amount of freshly ground white pepper. Toss gently, adding a little more cooking water if necessary.

Divide the pasta evenly into soup plates. Sprinkle each with 2 tablespoons cheese. Do not mix. Drizzle with a little additional truffle oil, if desired.

Serves 4

GRAPENOTE

This deserves a great Tuscan red like Sassicaia, but it also would be quite thrilling with a weighty Italian white like Mastroberardino's Greco di Tufo.

A Very Old Neapolitan Recipe: Macaroni and Tomatoes

ADD-ONS

Add ⅓ cup freshly grated Parmigiano-Reggiano to the hot pasta and toss.

GRAPENOTE

Try a bottle of Chianti Classico from a favorite producer.

Time lends enchantment to many dishes. This recipe was found by Italian cooking master Giuliano Bugialli in an Italian cookbook from 1841. Naples is famous as the home of the pizza, but it's also the home of this fascinating pasta. Giuliano suggests a short tubular pasta, but I like the charm of cavatelli.

8 ounces dried cavatelli

6 tablespoons olive oil

1 (28-ounce) can imported plum tomatoes in puree

Preheat the oven to 400°.

In a medium bowl, mix the pasta and the olive oil. Let the pasta soak in the oil for 20 minutes.

Add tomatoes and puree to pasta. Add 1 teaspoon coarse salt and freshly ground black pepper to taste and mix well.

Transfer the pasta to a large, shallow casserole brushed with a little olive oil. Bake 45 minutes, mixing several times during baking to prevent the pasta from sticking to casserole. Serve immediately.

Serves 2 to 3

Spinach Fettuccine with Tomato Butter

Never did such a little can produce a big sauce with such tomatoey intensity. This takes only minutes to make and will become your favorite emergency meal.

> 6 ounces good-quality tomato paste
>
> ½ cup (1 stick) unsalted butter
>
> 12 ounces fresh spinach fettuccine

Put the tomato paste in a heavy small saucepan and add ¼ cup water. Heat gently. Cut the butter into small pieces and add to the tomato mixture. Stir with a wooden spoon over low heat until the butter is incorporated. Season with salt and pepper to taste.

In a large pot of boiling water, cook the spinach fettuccine until it is tender. This will take only a few minutes. Do not overcook. Drain in a colander, saving 3 tablespoons of cooking liquid. Add the reserved cooking water to the tomato sauce and heat gently.

Place the pasta on a large, warm platter and spoon the hot tomato sauce over the top.

Serves 4

ADD-ONS

Add freshly grated Grana Padano on top of the pasta. Grana Padano is a cheese similar to Parmigiano-Reggiano made near Parma.

GRAPENOTE

A bottle of Antinori Galestro will make a modest dish seem less so.

Penne and Pencil Asparagus, Torta di Mascarpone

ADD-ONS

Garnish with julienned basil or lightly toasted pignoli.

GRAPENOTE

This dish can handle a variety of wine partners, white or red. Try an assertive sauvignon blanc from Italy, or a bright young nebbiolo from the Valtellina region.

This is one of the first dishes I created using only three ingredients. Its delicious simplicity led to the development of an entire new repertoire of recipes.

Small cubes of torta di mascarpone—a layered loaf of mascarpone, provolone, and basil—melt miraculously into a creamy, flavorful sauce. You can find it in cheese shops and specialty-food stores.

8 ounces penne or ziti (#2)

8 ounces thin asparagus, cut on the diagonal into 1¼-inch lengths

12 ounces torta di mascarpone, cut into small pieces

Bring a large pot of salted water to a boil. Add the penne and cook 8 minutes, or until it is just beginning to get tender. Add the asparagus pieces and cook 2 minutes, or until the asparagus and the pasta are both al dente. Drain the pasta well, saving ⅓ cup of the cooking water.

Put the hot cooking water in the bottom of a large warmed bowl. Add the drained pasta and asparagus. Add the torta di mascarpone and stir gently with a wooden spoon until the cheese melts completely. Season with salt and freshly ground pepper to taste.

Serves 4

Chapter 9

Main Courses

*O*nce upon a time the word "gourmet" referred to those apt to judge a meal for its elaborateness rather than by the quality of its food. One of the goals of *Recipes 1-2-3* is to redefine the gourmet as one who demands quality and respects the clarity of simple flavors.

Especially when it comes to the heart of the meal.

Although strongly infused with the flavors of the Mediterranean (my style of cooking for over a decade), these main courses reflect the hybridization of the American kitchen—where the exotic becomes familiar and sophistication becomes comfortable.

Steamed Clams in Thyme Butter

I ate this memorable dish while on a consulting trip to Paris. Restaurant Le Duc on Boulevard Raspail was known for its all-seafood menu, impressive with its selection of twenty-six fish entrées and more than a dozen choices of crustaceans. My favorite: Poulardes Sautées au Thym.

4 quarts littleneck clams (about 5 dozen)

½ cup (1 stick) unsalted butter

1 large bunch fresh thyme

Scrub the clams well and wash them thoroughly. Soak them in a cold brine of ⅓ cup salt to 1 gallon of water for 30 minutes. Wash again.

Melt the butter in a large heavy pot with a tightly fitting cover. Add ½ cup water, 3 tablespoons fresh thyme leaves, 1 teaspoon whole black peppercorns, and 1½ teaspoons coarse salt. Add the clams, cover, and cook over high heat 6 to 8 minutes, until shells open. Shake pan back and forth to cook clams evenly.

Remove from the heat the moment the shells open. Pour the clams, shells, and broth into heated bowls. Serve immediately.

Serves 4 to 6

ADD-ONS

Serve with small steamed red potatoes or with garlic bread.

GRAPENOTE

Classic with a bottle of chilled Muscadet "Sur Lie" or Picpoul de Pinet, a crisp white wine that is enormously popular in Paris.

Barbecue Pepper Shrimp

This is a New Orleans–style recipe that has nothing to do with an outdoor barbecue. Serve with Bay-Smoked Potatoes (page 195) or chili-spiked pasta for a great flavor match.

> 2 pounds large shrimp, in their shells
>
> 1 cup butter (2 sticks), cold, cut into small pieces
>
> 3 tablespoons Worcestershire sauce

Preheat the oven to 400°.

Wash the shrimp and peel them, leaving the tails on. Make a cut along the back of each shrimp and rinse under cold water to remove the vein. Dry on paper towels.

Place the shrimp in a single layer in a shallow casserole with ¼ cup crushed black peppercorns. Top with the butter. Bake 5 minutes.

Toss the shrimp, then add the Worcestershire sauce and 2 teaspoons coarse salt. Bake 2 minutes longer.

Put under the broiler for 1 minute. Remove and serve in soup plates with the pan juices.

Serves 5 to 6

ADD-ONS

Squeeze the juice of 2 lemons over the top.

GRAPENOTE

Try an aggressively varietal sauvignon blanc from South Africa, like Thelema— or Brander, from the Santa Ynez area of California.

Tuna Burgers, Hoisin, and Pickled Ginger

At the Rainbow Room, where I am consulting chef, members of the Rockefeller Center Club have been eating tuna burgers with great relish. Or rather, with pickled ginger. They like it seared rare, sitting on a bed of spicy gingered coleslaw. No one asks for ketchup . . . or even a hamburger bun!

2 pounds fresh tuna, skin and bones removed

6 tablespoons hoisin sauce

6 tablespoons Japanese pickled ginger (see Sources, page 290), kimchee, or Red Onion Salad (page 132)

Mince the tuna very fine with a sharp knife, or grind it in a meat grinder (you can ask your fish store to do this). The tuna should resemble chopped meat. Season with 1½ teaspoons coarse salt and freshly ground black pepper to taste. Form into 6 thick patties. Chill until ready to use.

Heat the hoisin sauce in a small saucepan with 2 tablespoons water. Keep warm.

Preheat the broiler. Broil the tuna burgers on both sides until the outside is browned and the inside is pink, about 6 minutes total.

Pour the warm sauce over the tuna and garnish with pickled ginger, kimchee, or Red Onion Salad. Serve with a fork and knife.

Serves 6

GRAPENOTE

This is a nice match with a not-too-sweet chilled white zinfandel from Dunnewood Vineyards, or Vin de Mistral Grenache Rosé from Joseph Phelps.

Red Snapper in Burnt Orange Oil

I use every edible part of the orange in this dish: juice—which emulsifies into a sauce—the segments for texture, and the peel for a heady aroma. These flavors enliven the sweet, fresh red snapper fillets, with dazzling results.

> 5 medium juice oranges, or blood oranges if available
>
> ½ cup olive oil or herb-flavored oil (basil, page 156, rosemary, sage)
>
> 4 red snapper fillets, 6 ounces each, skin removed

Wash the oranges. With a vegetable peeler, remove 8 long strips of orange zest and reserve. Make sure to remove any white pith. Cut the rind completely off 4 oranges. Cut the oranges between the membranes to make segments, being careful to remove all membrane. Reserve.

Heat the oil in large nonstick skillet. Add the strips of orange zest. Just as they become dark brown, remove and reserve.

Sprinkle salt and pepper on both sides of the fish. Add to the hot oil and sauté on both sides until crisp and lightly browned (you may need to do this in two batches). Remove the cooked fish to a warm platter.

Add the orange segments and the juice of the remaining orange (just cut in half and squeeze) to the oil in the pan. Cook over high heat for 1 minute, add salt and pepper to taste, and pour over the fish. Garnish with the burnt orange peel.

Serves 4

ADD-ONS

In the oil in the pan, fry paper-thin slices of raw carrot (sliced lengthwise) until crisp. Serve with the fish.

GRAPENOTE

Open a bottle of chardonnay from Australia—Rosemount Estate or Lindemans—or Beringer reserve from California.

Crispy Salmon with Pancetta and Sage

ADD-ONS

Drinking red? Try White Polenta with Parmigiano-Reggiano (page 189). Drinking white? Serve with Chardonnay Cabbage (page 198) or Potato-Fennel Mash (page 190).

GRAPENOTES

The full meaty flavor of the fish will go beautifully with a California chardonnay or a medium-bodied pinot noir with a hint of spice and oak in its finish.

Red wine with fish? You bet. This sophisticated confluence of flavors makes the much-loved salmon worthy of a great pinot noir. White wine with fish? Yes! A big chardonnay, if you serve this crispy salmon on a bed of buttery braised cabbage.

4 thick salmon fillets, 6 ounces each, cut from the center of fish

8 ounces thinly sliced pancetta

24 leaves fresh sage

Remove the skin and with tweezers all the small bones from the salmon. Holding a sharp knife on the bias, cut 2 deep slits across the width of each piece of fish. Do not cut all the way through. You will have 2 "pockets" in each piece.

Lay the pancetta flat in a large nonstick skillet. Cook over low heat until most of fat is rendered and the pancetta is just beginning to crisp. Remove the pancetta with tongs and let it cool 5 minutes. Reserve the rendered fat.

Place the pancetta and 3 sage leaves in each slit, allowing the edges of the sage and pancetta to show. Heat the fat in a skillet. Season the fish with salt and pepper and place, slit side down, in the skillet. Cook over medium heat until the fish begins to brown and get crisp. Turn the fillets and finish cooking to desired doneness. The fish should be crisp on the outside, moist on the inside.

Serves 4

Roast Cod with Red Pepper Puree

You might use roasted fresh peppers for this dish with good results, but I love the tingle of vinegar in the sauce, so I keep a jar of roasted red peppers on my shelf for a luxurious and quick dish. Buy thick, fleshy cod fillets.

4 cod fillets, 6 ounces each

1 (12-ounce) jar of roasted red peppers

¼ cup (½ stick) unsalted butter, cold

Preheat the oven to 375°.

Dust the cod fillets with salt and freshly ground white pepper. Set aside.

Puree the roasted peppers with their liquid in a food processor until smooth and thick. Transfer to a small, heavy pot.

In large, ovenproof skillet, melt ½ tablespoon of the butter. Sauté the fish briefly on each side and put it in the oven for 8 to 10 minutes. When it's done, the fish will flake easily, but do not overcook.

Heat the red pepper puree until very hot. Remove from the heat. Whisk in the remaining cold butter and stir until smooth (sauce yields about 1½ cups). Keep warm.

Remove the fish from the oven, pour any juices into the red pepper sauce, and mix.

Pool ⅓ cup sauce on the bottom of each plate. Place the fish on top.

Serves 4

ADD-ONS

Serve with Braised Celery Batons, Fried Celery Leaves (page 204).

GRAPENOTE

Lovely match with an Anjou Blanc from the Loire Valley to balance the sweetness and acidity in the dish.

Rosemary-Infused Swordfish

Swordfish has a special affinity for rosemary and garlic. In addition to its very Mediterranean flavors, this dish is a low-calorie joy, because it dry-cooks in the pan. Use ultra-fresh fish.

2 large cloves garlic, very finely minced

2 tablespoons fresh rosemary, finely minced

1½ pounds swordfish, cut into 4 steaks

In a small bowl, mix the garlic, 1½ teaspoons butcher-grind black pepper, 1½ teaspoons coarse salt, and the rosemary until you have a coarse paste. A mortar and pestle is ideal. Spread the mixture evenly on both sides of the fish. Let sit 1 hour.

Heat a nonstick skillet or grill pan until hot. Cook the swordfish 3 to 4 minutes over medium-high heat on each side until browned and lightly caramelized.

Serves 4

ADD-ONS

You can add 2 tablespoons olive oil while the fish is marinating, or drizzle extra-virgin olive oil on top of the fish after cooking. Pass fresh lemon wedges and garnish with fresh rosemary sprigs. Delicious with Cumin-Scented Couscous (page 212) and Slow-Roasted Romas (page 220).

GRAPENOTES

A special match with Rabbit Ridge viognier, provençal white Cassis, or a more unusual Châteauneuf-du-Pape Blanc from France.

Pepper-Seared Tuna, Cool Mango Relish

Sales of fish and seafood have risen more than 25 percent in the last ten years. Just wait until people start eating this dish—mango sales will also soar! Together these flavors are a singular sensation.

> 2 ripe mangoes
>
> 6 tablespoons chopped fresh cilantro, plus whole leaves for garnish
>
> 4 fresh tuna steaks, 6 ounces each

About 1 hour before serving, peel the mangoes with a sharp knife. Cut the flesh away from the pit, dice it into ¼-inch pieces, and put it in a small bowl. Add the chopped cilantro and a pinch of salt and mix well. Chill for 30 minutes.

Lightly press ½ teaspoon butcher-grind black pepper into one side of each tuna steak. Sprinkle lightly with salt. Place the fish, pepper side down, in a large nonstick skillet. Cook on both sides over medium-high heat until the fish is seared on the outside but still pink in the center. Cut the tuna on the bias with a sharp knife into ½-inch-thick slices.

Mound mango relish in the center of each plate. Arrange the tuna slices, overlapping, to form a circle around the relish. Garnish with fresh cilantro leaves.

Serves 4

ADD-ONS

Serve with wedges of fresh lime. Also delicious atop Red Onion Salad (page 132).

GRAPENOTE

The appealing fruit, perfume, and acidity of the South African sauvignon blanc from Mulderbosch make this fish dish sing.

Red Onion Salad

This sprightly onion salad is one of the most enticing relishes I've ever had. It's the balance of vinegar and sweetness that makes my mouth water. Toss with a couple of pounds of large chilled shrimp for a fabulous first course. Or serve atop salads, sandwiches, grilled fish, poultry, steaks . . .

1 pound medium-size red onions
1 cup tarragon vinegar
½ cup sugar

Peel the onions, slice them into ¼-inch-thick rings, and put them in a large jar. Pour in 1 cup water, the vinegar, the sugar, ½ teaspoon black peppercorns, and ¼ teaspoon coarse salt. Cover tightly and shake well until the sugar is dissolved. Store in the refrigerator. Let marinate, refrigerated, one day before serving.

Makes 3 cups

Steamed Halibut, Bell Pepper Confetti

Most of the halibut we eat comes from the Pacific, and it is known as "the hippo of the sea." I'm especially fond of the way the brightly colored peppers contrast with the snowy whiteness of the fish. Halibut is caught only during a few 24-hour periods in May and June, the perfect time for this dish.

2 each: yellow and red bell peppers

¼ cup olive oil or Garlic Oil (page 52), plus 2
   tablespoons for oiling the fish

4 halibut steaks, 6 ounces each

To make the bell pepper confetti: Cut the peppers meticulously into little ⅓-inch squares. Place them in a small nonstick skillet with the ¼ cup oil. Add ½ teaspoon coarse salt and ¼ teaspoon whole black peppercorns. Cover and simmer over very low heat for 10 minutes, or until the peppers are tender.

Brush the halibut with a little oil and season with salt and freshly ground white pepper. Steam in a large pan fitted with a steamer basket until the fish is cooked to the desired degree of doneness—about 10 minutes, depending on thickness. Pour "confetti" over the fish and serve immediately.

Serves 4

ADD-ONS

Serve with lemon wedges. Shower with julienned basil or flat parsley. Or add 1 teaspoon fennel seed to the peppers while cooking.

GRAPENOTE

These clean flavors call for a medium-bodied white with well-balanced acidity. Try a chardonnay with finesse, either from California or Italy. Also great with Pinot d'Alsace from Domaine Zind-Humbrecht.

Salmon Baked in Grape Leaves

Oh, is this good! Salmon bakes in an ancestral "wrap" of briny grape leaves, softened with a bit of butter. Keep the grape leaves on the fish when you serve it—they are delicious. This is pure Med-Rim when served with Fried Lemon and Zucchini Salad. It is also a wonderful way to prepare halibut fillets.

> **4 thick salmon fillets, 6 ounces each, cut from the center of the fish**
>
> **5 tablespoons unsalted butter**
>
> **8 large grape leaves in brine**

Preheat the oven to 450°.

Remove the skin and any bones from the fish. Season well with salt and pepper. Slice the butter thinly and place ½ tablespoon on top of each fillet.

Remove the grape leaves from their brine and pat dry with paper towels. Wrap the fish tightly in grape leaves, using 2 for each piece of fish. Tuck in the ends of the grape leaves to make a tight, neat package.

Spread 2 tablespoons of the remaining butter over the bottom of a baking pan. Use bits of the remaining butter (1 tablespoon) to cover the tops of the grape leaf–wrapped fish.

Put the fish on the baking sheet and bake 8 minutes. Serve the fish immediately, still wrapped in the grape leaves.

Serves 4

Serve with Fried Lemon and Zucchini Salad (page 178), or Cumin-Scented Couscous (page 212).

GRAPENOTE

A glass of Marsanne, a Rhône white, would be a refreshing accompaniment to the light, smoky flavor of the fish. Or as an alternative, a light-bodied Greek red would take your palate in a surprising direction.

Pan-Seared Tuna Niçoise, Tomato "Water"

A chic version of the more traditional salade niçoise, this is made with fresh rosy-pink tuna topped with a salad of julienned tomato and oil-cured olives—the signature components. Natural tomato juices become the dressing. Serve with Parmesan Lace Galettes and you'll have a riot of flavors, textures, and temperatures.

6 large, ripe tomatoes

36 oil-cured black olives

4 fresh tuna steaks, 6 ounces each

One to two hours before serving, trim off the outer wall of the tomatoes with a small, sharp knife. Remove the pulp from inside the tomato and reserve. Cut the wall into thin julienned strips ⅛ inch wide by 1½ inches long. Pit the olives and cut them in half. Put the tomato julienne and olives in a small bowl with ½ teaspoon coarse salt. Let sit for 30 minutes at room temperature.

Coarsely chop the reserved pulp of the tomatoes, removing any seeds. Put in a blender at high speed and process until you have a smooth puree. Reserve.

Sprinkle the tuna lightly with white pepper and salt. Heat a large nonstick skillet and sear the tuna on both sides until browned but still pink inside.

Spoon the tomato water on the bottom at 4 large plates. Place the cooked fish on sauce and top with the tomato-olive mixture.

Serves 4

ADD-ONS

Garnish with finely chopped egg white. Serve with thinly sliced Bay-Smoked Potatoes (page 195) and steamed haricots verts. Or serve with Parmesan Lace Galettes (page 49).

GRAPENOTE

Try a well-chilled off-dry rosé like Tavel, or a white Bordeaux such as Château Bonnet, to complement this dish's sunny flavors.

Two-Way Salmon and Zucchini

Three simple ingredients can make two dramatically different styles of fish: poached and pan-seared, plus two "gourmet" sauces: a dark zucchini coulis and a creamy zucchini butter sauce. This is the magic of Recipes 1-2-3.

1 Poached Salmon with Zucchini, Two Sauces

1½ pounds medium-size zucchini

4 salmon fillets, 6 ounces each

2 tablespoons unsalted butter, cold

Cut one-sixth of the zucchini into paper-thin rounds. Place in an overlapping pattern on top of the fish. Sprinkle with salt and freshly ground white pepper and wrap each piece tightly in plastic wrap. Refrigerate 30 minutes.

Cut the remaining zucchini in half lengthwise and then across into ½-inch pieces. Put in a medium-size pot with ½ cup water and ½ teaspoon salt. Bring to a boil, lower the heat, cover, and cook 15 minutes, or until the zucchini is very soft.

Meanwhile, unwrap the salmon and poach in a shallow pan in 1 inch of water until cooked through. (You can also steam the fish in the plastic wrap in a steamer.)

Transfer one-half of the cooked zucchini and one-half of the cooking liquid to a blender and puree until smooth. Reserve. Transfer remaining zucchini and liquid to the blender and puree until smooth. Add the butter and puree until thick and creamy.

You will now have two sauces—a dark-green coulis (with no butter) and a light, creamy sauce with butter.

GRAPENOTE

Serve with a full-bodied California chardonnay or French white Burgundy. From California, try Château Woltner—from France, a Montagny.

To serve, place ¼ cup of the dark sauce on the bottom of each of 4 plates. Top each with a warm poached salmon fillet and put 2 tablespoons of the buttery sauce over the top of each.

II *Pan-Seared Salmon, Creamy Zucchini Sauce*

8 ounces zucchini

4 salmon fillets, 6 ounces each

2 tablespoons unsalted butter, cold, cut into a few pieces

Cut the zucchini into large chunks and put in a small pot. Cook in ¼ cup water with ¼ teaspoon salt until very soft.

Meanwhile, season the salmon with salt and pepper and sear in a nonstick skillet on both sides until medium-rare. Keep warm.

As soon as the zucchini is soft, transfer the contents of the pot to a blender. Blend until smooth and creamy. Add the butter. Blend again—sauce will lighten in color and thicken. Add salt and pepper to taste. Pour the hot sauce immediately around the salmon.

I, II: Serves 4

GRAPENOTES

Because you have seared the fish, this preparation will lend itself beautifully to a lighter-style pinot noir, or a cru Beaujolais.

Perfect Chicken Salad

Once you use this method of poaching whole chicken, you will never make it any other way, for the meat has a remarkable velvety texture. As a bonus, you can reduce the broth to use as a base for restorative chicken soup. Cut the chicken into small dice for sandwiches; julienne into long, thin strips for main-course salads.

2½-pound whole chicken

1 cup chopped celery

1 cup mayonnaise or Flavored Mayonnaise (page 139)

Wash and clean the chicken. Bring 4 quarts of water to boil in a large pot. Submerge the chicken and boil quietly, uncovered, for 15 minutes.

Turn off the heat, cover, and let the chicken remain in the water for 30 minutes.

Remove from the water and reserve the broth for another use. Pull out as many bones as possible and refrigerate the chicken until cold. Remove all bones and skin. Cut chicken into ½-inch chunks.

Toss with the celery and mayonnaise. Chill. Makes about 2 pounds.

Serves 6

ADD-ONS

Serve on a platter lined with soft green lettuce, together with Red Onion Salad (page 132) and ripe cherry tomatoes.

GRAPENOTE

Try a chilled dry riesling from Hermann Weimer from the Finger Lakes, Upstate New York, or an easy-drinking dry chenin blanc from Chappellet, in California.

Flavored Mayonnaises I-II-III

I *Anchovy-Lemon Mayonnaise*

1 cup light mayonnaise
1 (2-ounce) can anchovies and capers in oil
Grated zest of 1 lemon and 1 tablespoon of lemon juice

Process all the ingredients in a blender until very smooth and creamy.
Add freshly ground black pepper to taste.

II *Sun-Dried Tomato Mayonnaise*

1 cup light mayonnaise
¼ cup sun-dried tomatoes in oil
1 clove garlic, pushed through a garlic press

Put all the ingredients in a food processor and puree until smooth and
creamy. Add freshly ground black pepper to taste.

III *Spicy Cilantro Mayonnaise*

1 cup light mayonnaise
2½ tablespoons finely chopped fresh cilantro
1 tablespoon minced pickled jalapeños

Combine all the ingredients in a small bowl and whisk until blended.

Each makes about 1 cup

Chicken Roasted in a Salt Crust

Copious amounts of coarse (kosher) salt form an impenetrable crust around the chicken in this dish, sealing in the natural juices and producing meltingly tender meat. Crack open the oven-baked igloo and herbal perfume will waft through your kitchen. Surprisingly, this ancient cooking method imparts a unique taste without excessive saltiness and is equally good (and dramatic) with whole red snapper.

1 whole 4-pound chicken, at room temperature

Large bunch fresh thyme (enough to fill the cavity of the chicken)

12 small new (or fingerling) potatoes

Preheat the oven to 450°.

Wash the chicken and pat it dry with paper towels. Fill the cavity with fresh thyme and season the skin with freshly ground black pepper.

Pour 3 cups kosher salt into the bottom of a deep ovenproof casserole or a pot with cover. Put the chicken on the salt, breast side up, and ring with the potatoes. Add salt to cover the top of the chicken (about 10 cups). Sprinkle with 1 cup water, patting the salt down to make a solid crust.

Bake, covered, for 45 minutes. Remove the cover and bake 20 minutes more. Remove from the oven and let rest 10 minutes.

Crack the salt crust with the back of a heavy knife. Remove the chicken and potatoes. Remove all the salt with a pastry brush or paper towel. Cut the chicken as desired. Serve with sprigs of thyme and the roasted new potatoes.

Serves 4 to 6

ADD-ONS

Before baking, rub the skin of the chicken with 2 cloves of garlic that have been pushed through a garlic press. Serve the chicken drizzled with ¼ cup fruity olive oil that has been gently warmed.

GRAPENOTE

Try a simple Mâcon or Saint-Veran if you want white, or a Beaujolais-Villages if you want red.

Poulet Rôti with Wild Mushrooms

Nothing is more satisfying than a classic roast chicken, and this version, sauced with woodsy porcini mushrooms, rules the roost.

1 whole 4-pound chicken

1 cup dried porcini mushrooms

1/4 cup (1/2 stick) unsalted butter, cold

Preheat the oven to 375°.

Wash the chicken and pat it dry with paper towels. Save the neck and gizzards, except for the liver. Salt and pepper the chicken evenly and sprinkle salt and pepper in the cavity.

Soak the dried porcini in 2 cups of very hot water for 20 minutes. Drain them, saving the soaking water. Sauté the mushrooms in 1 tablespoon of the butter for 3 to 4 minutes. Fill the cavity of the chicken with the sautéed mushrooms. Truss the chicken and rub it with a tablespoon of butter. Place the chicken in a heavy, shallow casserole and roast for 1 to 1¼ hours, basting often.

Meanwhile, put the gizzards and the neck in a small pot with ½ cup water and the mushroom liquid, strained through a fine sieve. Bring to a boil, lower the heat, and simmer 20 to 25 minutes, until the liquid is reduced to 1¼ cups. Pour the liquid through a strainer and discard the gizzards and neck.

Remove chicken from the oven, untruss, and put on a platter. Scoop the mushrooms out of the chicken and put them in the roasting pan with the reduced mushroom juices. Reduce by one-third. Add salt and pepper to taste and whisk in 2 tablespoons cold butter until the sauce emulsifies. Cut the chicken as desired and cover with the wild mushroom sauce.

Serves 4 to 6

Add ¼ cup ruby port to the juices in the roasting pan while reducing. A wonderful accompaniment to this classic preparation is Gratin Dauphinoise (page 192).

GRAPENOTE

A velvety, easy-drinking merlot would be a lovely way to integrate the flavors and body of this dish. If white is more to your liking, now's a good time to remember what great Burgundy is all about.

Country-Fried Chicken

When at the age of twenty-three I was first chef to New York's Mayor Ed Koch, Hizzoner selected the menu for my cooking debut, a dinner party for the Council of East Coast Mayors. Green salad, fried chicken, chocolate mousse. Little did I know this was the unofficial beginning of Recipes 1-2-3.

2 frying chickens, cut into eight pieces each

4 cups self-rising flour

2 cups solid vegetable shortening

Put the chicken parts in a large bowl. Fill with cold water and refrigerate overnight (or for 12 hours). Pat the chicken pieces completely dry and lightly salt each piece. Mix the flour with 1 tablespoon freshly ground black pepper. Dredge each piece in the flour-pepper mixture.

  Heat 1 cup of the shortening in each of two large heavy frying pans. Add the chicken pieces, skin side down, and fry for 10 minutes. Cover and fry for 10 minutes more. Adjust the heat during cooking so the chicken continues to sizzle without spattering. Turn the chicken, cover, and cook 10 more minutes. Turn the chicken again and cook uncovered 5 minutes, or until the chicken is crisp and the juices run clear.

Serves 8

ADD-ONS

Add a pinch of cinnamon, thyme, or nutmeg to the flour. Instead of water, you can soak the chicken in buttermilk. Or double-dip: After the first dip in seasoned flour, dip in the buttermilk, then in the flour again. Serve with green Tabasco.

GRAPENOTE

Choose a delightful Pheasant Ridge chenin blanc from Texas. I also like a fruity red wine, such as dolcetto or young Chianti, for an upbeat contrast and a good way to cut through the fat.

Chicken-in-a-Watermelon

Fairly sweet and succulent, this improbable dish will make a big hit on April Fools' Day, a holiday strangely bereft of a single signature dish. It makes a spectacular, if fairly alarming, presentation on a silver tray.

1 very large watermelon

Roaster chicken, about 5 to 6 pounds

1 tablespoon five-spice powder

Preheat the oven to 400°.

Cut a ¼-inch-thick horizontal slice off one long side of the watermelon and discard it. Cut off the top third of the melon horizontally. Core and seed both parts of the melon, making room for the chicken. Season the cavity of chicken with salt and freshly ground black pepper. Rub the skin of chicken with the five-spice powder.

Place the chicken in the larger portion of the melon and then place the other piece of melon on top, securing it with long skewers. Put a baking pan on the bottom rack of the oven to catch any juices. Bake the watermelon directly on the rack above for 2 hours at 400° and then 2½ hours at 300°.

Very carefully place the watermelon on a tray and present it to your guests. Return to the kitchen to remove the chicken from the watermelon and carve it. Remove the juices from the watermelon and reduce them in a skillet until thickened.

Serves 6 to 8

ADD-ONS

Whisk 3 tablespoons cold unsalted butter into juices while reducing them in the skillet. For extra flavor, add 1 tablespoon fresh lemon juice or soy sauce.

GRAPENOTE

A remarkable contrast with a not-too-sweet white zinfandel from California.

Chicken "Villagio," Diced Lemon Sauce

ADD-ONS

Garnish with julienned basil leaves or strips of roasted red or yellow pepper.

GRAPENOTE

Perfect with San Anselmi, a single-vineyard soave, or Vernaccia di San Gimignano, if you're drinking white; or try a Montepulciano d'Abruzzo if you're drinking red.

This inventive, rustic dish is characterized by strong, definitive flavors. Italians would serve it with la scarpetta ("the slipper"), a piece of bread for mopping up the delicious juices. Accompany with creamy White Polenta with Parmigiano-Reggiano (page 189) and a sturdy Italian wine.

> 8 chicken thighs (about 2½ pounds)
> 3 medium-size lemons
> 6 ounces pepperoni (1-inch-diameter sausage)

Trim any excess fat from the chicken. Put the chicken in a ceramic bowl. Grate the zest of the two lemons on the medium-size holes of a box grater. Save the lemons. Add the rind to the chicken, along with ½ teaspoon coarse salt and ¼ teaspoon butcher-grind black pepper. Slice the pepperoni into ¼-inch-thick rounds. Add to the chicken, mix well, and marinate several hours or overnight.

Cut the pith away from the lemons with a sharp knife. Make sure all of the white membrane is removed. Cut lemon flesh into ¼-inch dice. Reserve.

Put the chicken, skin side down, in a large nonstick skillet, along with pepperoni. Cook over medium heat until the chicken is golden and turn over. Continue to cook and turn until the chicken is done and the sausage is browned. This will take about 20 minutes. Add the diced lemon and continue to cook, 3 to 4 minutes more. The lemon will thicken the pan juices. Add salt and pepper to taste.

Transfer to a large platter with a slotted spoon. Serve piping hot.

Serves 4

Yogurt Chicken with Blackened Onions

The onion-and-yogurt marinade tenderizes chicken to satiny perfection. For an unusual flavor match, try this with Barley-Buttermilk Salad, flecked with cilantro. This dish feels like summer.

8 chicken thighs (about 2½ pounds)

1½ cups plain yogurt

1 cup onions chopped into ⅛-inch dice

Remove any excess fat from the chicken. Put the chicken in a medium nonmetallic bowl with the yogurt and diced onions. Add ½ teaspoon salt and mix well. Cover and refrigerate overnight.

Preheat the oven to 350°.

Place the chicken pieces in a metal baking pan, making sure the pieces are separated and well covered with yogurt and onions. Bake for 40 minutes. Then broil the chickens, with the pan set at the greatest distance from heat, until onions are somewhat blackened. Be careful not to let them burn completely. This will take 4 to 5 minutes. Sprinkle with ½ teaspoon salt. Serve hot or cold.

Serves 4

ADD-ONS

Serve with Barley-Buttermilk Salad (page 194). Shower with freshly chopped cilantro or ground sumac.

GRAPENOTE

An interesting and refreshing match with a rosé wine—such as Vin Gris de Cigare, from Bonny Doon of California.

Cornish Hen Under a Brick

You really need a brick or two for making this dish, because the authentic northern Italian preparation, mattone *(the word for heavy brick), requires that the hen lie completely flat while cooking. Ultra-crisp skin and succulent meat will have you licking your fingers.*

ADD-ONS

Add 1 tablespoon chopped fresh rosemary to the pan while reducing the wine.

GRAPENOTE

Try a Dolcetto d'Alba for an authentic flavor match, or drink the white wine you've cooked with—perhaps an Italian pinot grigio from Bollini or a white from Orvieto.

1½-pound cornish hen

3 tablespoons Garlic Oil (page 52)—plus additional for drizzling, if desired

½ cup dry white wine

With kitchen shears, cut the hen along the length of the backbone. With your fist, pound the bird flat so that it is butterflied. Season with salt and pepper.

Heat the oil in a large nonstick skillet. Place the hen, skin side down, in the oil and place a brick wrapped in aluminum foil on top. Cook over medium heat, turning every 2 to 3 minutes, for 10 minutes, or until golden brown.

Remove the hen to a large warm plate. Add the wine to the pan and reduce over high heat, scraping up the browned bits in the pan. When the sauce has thickened, pour it over the hen. Serve immediately. Drizzle with additional garlic oil if desired.

Serves 1 or 2

Brine-Cured Cornish Hens,
Glazed Shallots and Parsnip Puree

This 1-2-3 dish is actually three recipes in one. Soaking these small birds (a breed of baby chicken) in brine makes them particularly moist and brings out their flavor. This is a lovely dish for company, especially when fall is in the air.

2 cornish hens, 1¼ pounds

16 medium-size shallots

1 pound parsnips

Wash the hens and sprinkle the cavities with kosher salt. Place them in a large bowl or plastic bucket and cover with cold water. Add 1 cup kosher salt and stir until the salt dissolves. Refrigerate for 6 hours, but not longer.

Parboil shallots for 5 minutes, then peel.

Preheat the oven to 350°.

Remove the hens from the brine and pat them dry with paper towels. Truss. Place them in a baking pan or shallow casserole. Grind a liberal amount of black pepper onto the skin of the hens. Surround hens with shallots. Put ¼ inch of water in the bottom of the pan. Bake for 45 minutes. Baste the hens, adding a little water to pan if necessary.

While the hens are baking, peel the parsnips and cut them into 2-inch pieces. Bring to a boil in salted water. Lower the heat and simmer 25 to 30 minutes, until the parsnips are very tender. Transfer them with a slotted spoon to a food processor or blender. Process until very smooth. Keep warm. You should have 1½ cups.

After the hens have baked for 45 minutes, put them under the

Try a full-bodied chardonnay with floral tones and a touch of oak. In winter, open a Châteauneuf-du-Pape.

broiler for 30 seconds to brown. Remove the hens and caramelized shallots from the broiler.

Spoon the parsnip puree onto the bottom of a serving platter. Cut hens in half, discarding string, and place atop puree along with the shallots.

Serves 4

The following photos depict:

Soups and Pasta:

1. An Unusual Borscht: Roasted Beet, Squash, and Yogurt

2. Cheese Raviolini, Roasted Pumpkin Sauce

3. Farfalle with Broccoli, Broccoli-Butter Sauce

4. Orecchiette with Endive and Sun-Dried Tomatoes

Main Courses:

5. Pepper-Seared Tuna, Cool Mango Relish

6. Crispy Salmon with Pancetta and Sage

7. Red Snapper in Burnt Orange Oil

8. Pan-Seared Tuna Niçoise, Tomato "Water"

9. One Duck, Two Dinners:

    Braised Duck Legs with Apples and Sauerkraut

    Sautéed Duck Breasts with Green Olives and Sweet Vermouth

10. Brine-Cured Cornish Hens, Glazed Shallots and Parsnip Puree

11. Chicken "Villagio," Diced Lemon Sauce

12. Mahogany Short Ribs

Vegetables and Side Dishes:

13. Turnip and Havarti Torte

14. Zucchini, Black Olive, and Tomato Compote

15. Sugar Snaps in Orange Butter; Orange and Gold Potato Puree, Sweet Potato Chips

16. Pan-Grilled Radicchio, Fried Rosemary; Crisp Eggplant Tassels

One Duck, Two Dinners

I Braised Duck Legs with Apples and Sauerkraut

If "poultry is to the cook what canvas is to the painter," as Brillat-Savarin said, then here's artistic proof: two completely different-tasting preparations, each with only three ingredients. Both recipes are duck soup, but follow the instructions carefully.

1 duckling, about five pounds

1 pound sauerkraut, packed in a plastic bag

2 large Granny Smith apples, unpeeled

Cut the duck into the following pieces: 2 breast halves (no bones); 2 legs (with thighs). Reserve.

Use the neck, back, wings, and gizzards (do not use the liver) to make a stock: Put the pieces in a medium-size heavy pot with about 4 cups of water, or to cover. Add 1 teaspoon whole black peppercorns. Simmer for 2 hours with the cover askew, then strain through a fine sieve. Return the stock to the pot and reduce slowly to 2 cups. Reserve the stock for use in both duck preparations.

Preheat the oven to 350°.

Cook the duck legs slowly, turning several times, in a large non-stick skillet for 10 minutes. Pour off the fat and reserve. The duck skin should be browned.

Drain the sauerkraut. Dice one apple into ¼-inch cubes, removing the seeds. Mix with the sauerkraut and put in the bottom of a shallow casserole. Add ⅓ teaspoon whole black peppercorns, ½ teaspoon coarse salt, and ½ cup duck stock. Place the duck legs on top and

ADD-ONS

Splash sauerkraut with white wine or gin before baking. Boil tiny white potatoes until almost done, then sauté in duck fat until crisp and serve with the duck.

GRAPENOTE

Chill a bottle of Alsatian sylvaner or gewürztraminer and enjoy the marriage of body and flavors. My husband likes this dish with an off-dry bubbly, some of which he reluctantly adds to the sauerkraut before baking.

bake 45 minutes. Pour 3 tablespoons duck fat over the duck and sauerkraut. Bake 15 minutes longer.

Cut the remaining apple into 10 to 12 wedges, removing the seeds. Heat 1 tablespoon duck fat in a small nonstick skillet and sauté the apples over high heat until browned and soft. Remove the casserole from the oven. Put the sauerkraut and the duck legs on a platter and top with the sautéed apple slices.

II Sautéed Duck Breasts with Green Olives and Sweet Vermouth

2 duck breast halves, bones removed

¼ cup sweet vermouth

½ cup French Picholine or Spanish green olives

Make several slashes in the skin of the duck. Season with coarse salt and freshly ground black pepper. Refrigerate several hours.

Put the duck breasts, skin side down, in a cold, large nonstick skillet and cook slowly over medium heat until the fat is rendered. Pour the fat off. Turn the duck over and continue to cook 5 to 6 minutes.

Preheat the broiler.

Add ¼ cup of the reserved duck stock, the vermouth, and the olives to the pan. Increase the heat and cook 2 to 3 minutes. Remove the duck to a shallow baking pan or heavy-gauge pie tin and place under the broiler to crisp the skin.

Reduce the juices in the pan until thickened. Place the duck breasts on a platter and pour the sauce and olives over the duck.

I, II: Serves 2

ADD-ONS

Serve on a puree of very buttery Perfect Mashed Potatoes (page 217), seasoned judiciously with freshly ground white pepper.

GRAPENOTE

The fragrant, briary fruit of a California or Oregon pinot noir makes a compelling match. Soft tannins and good acidity do nice things for the duck.

Michael's Perfect Roast Turkey with Lemon and Sage

My husband—food and restaurant consultant by day, intellectual smartass by night—devised this solution to the age-old dilemma of dry breast meat or undercooked leg meat. "Ignore the darned popup timer," he says. "It guarantees an overcooked bird. Invest instead in a good meat thermometer." This is a wordy but worthy recipe.

> **16- to 18-pound fresh turkey, bought from your butcher, at room temperature**
>
> **2 tablespoons dried sage leaves (see Note)**
>
> **2 large lemons**

Preheat the oven to 325°.

Remove the fat from the rear of the turkey. Melt it in a small non-stick pan. Set aside.

Starting at the neck of the turkey, slip your fingers under the skin and carefully separate the skin from one entire side of the breast; most of your hand eventually will be under the skin. Continue downward and, with your index finger, separate the skin around the thigh. Repeat on the other side of the bird.

Crumble the sage leaves and sprinkle them with freshly ground black pepper. Spread 1 tablespoon of sage on breast and thigh, beneath the skin, on each half of the turkey. Prick each lemon several times and insert in the bird's cavity.

Put the neck and giblets in a baking pan; do not use liver. With a pastry brush, thoroughly coat the breast with the rendered fat, then sprinkle the entire bird with more pepper. Fold a double thickness of paper towels in half and cover the entire breast. Carefully pour cold

ADD-ONS

Add white wine to pan juices before reducing. Serve with Wild Rice and Bulghur Toss (page 203) and Cranberry Chutney (page 286).

GRAPENOTE

Your choice: From an oaky Washington State chardonnay, to French Beaujolais, elegant Oregon pinot noir, or vibrant California zinfandel.

water on the towels to thoroughly moisten them, then cover the breast area with an aluminum-foil tent. Place the bird on a rack over the gizzards and put it in the oven.

Every 20 minutes, pull the turkey from the oven, remove the foil tent, and thoroughly moisten the paper towels with cold water. Some water will flow into the pan and into the turkey; it will become part of your pan juices.

After 2½ hours, check the turkey temperature with a meat thermometer; the thigh should be about 145° and the breast 125°. If they are not, continue to cook (cooking time will depend on the initial temperature and on the size of the bird).

If they are, remove the foil and the paper towels and return the turkey to the oven for about 45 minutes. The breast will brown and temperatures will be 175° to 180° in the thigh and 155° to 160° in the breast.

Take the turkey out of the oven and remove the lemons. Tip the liquid inside the turkey into the roasting pan and then transfer all the pan juices and brown bits to a saucepan. Let the turkey rest under the foil tent. Skim the fat from the saucepan. Add ½ tablespoon juice from one of roasted lemons and bring to a boil. You should have about 1½ cups of liquid; either add water or reduce the liquid accordingly. Carve the turkey and serve with the pan juices.

Serves 12 to 14

Note: Buy whole dried sage leaves from a Middle Eastern or spice store (see Sources, page 289). Spice Islands is an adequate alternative. Do not use powdered sage.

Veal Roast with Leeks and Rosé Wine

When you want a meal that is comforting but impressive, try this. A rump roast of veal or a rolled and tied boneless veal shoulder are cuts that are often ignored. Slow braising, on a bed of leeks and in vapors of rosé wine, yields a very tender roast with a delicate flavor.

> **2 pounds rump roast of veal, or boneless veal shoulder rolled and tied**
>
> **6 large leeks**
>
> **1 cup dry French rosé wine.**

Preheat the oven to 350°.

Rub salt and freshly ground black pepper into the surface of the veal.

Trim off the green part of the leeks and reserve. Slice the white part of the leeks lengthwise and wash carefully. Cut into ½-inch slices. Put the leeks in the bottom of a large heavy casserole.

Sear the veal quickly on all sides in a nonstick pan. Place the veal on top of the leeks. Add ¼ cup water to the pan, bring to a boil, and scrape the pan with a wooden spoon. Pour the pan liquid and the wine into the casserole. Cover and cook 1 hour at 350°. Reduce the heat to 300° and cook 1¼ hours longer, or until very tender. Remove the meat. Let rest while you prepare the sauce. If desired, cut the green part of the leeks into diamond shapes and boil 2 to 3 minutes. Use as a garnish.

Puree half the leeks in a blender on low speed, adding enough pan juices to make a thick sauce. If necessary, add water. Process until very smooth. Pass the sauce through a coarse sieve. Add salt to taste. Slice the meat and serve it over a mound of the remaining leeks. Cover with sauce and garnish with diamond-shaped leeks.

Serves 4 to 6

ADD-ONS

Sprinkle the sauce with pink peppercorns. Serve with Perfect Mashed Potatoes (page 217).

GRAPENOTE

Serve with the same French (or Spanish) rosé that was used to cook the veal.

Osso Buco with Tomatoes and Black Olives

ADD-ONS

Sprinkle with Gremolata 1-2-3. Mix together:

1 tablespoon grated fresh lemon zest

1 teaspoon freshly minced garlic

3 tablespoons finely chopped parsley

GRAPENOTE

A velvety Tignanello from Italy, or a Barbaresco with some bottle age, would be mouthwatering mates.

A riff on the traditional Milanese dish, my osso buco (literally "bone with a hole") is based on only three ingredients: shanks of milk-fed veal, imported canned tomatoes, and oil-cured olives. Another twist is the coupling of this fork-tender veal with saffron orzo (instead of traditional rice). What remains the same is the standard add-on of gremolata: grated lemon zest, garlic, and parsley—another quick "1-2-3."

> 4 osso buco (veal shanks cut into 2-inch-thick pieces, bone marrow in center), about 3 pounds
>
> 1 (28-ounce) can plum tomatoes in puree, ½ cup reserved for another use
>
> ½ cup oil-cured black olives

In a large nonstick skillet, brown the shanks for 3 to 4 minutes on each side. Remove the meat, pour ½ cup water into the pan, and boil until reduced to ¼ cup.

Place the browned meat in a heavy shallow casserole. Pour the pan liquid, the tomatoes, and the puree over the top of the meat. Scatter the olives over the juices. Cover the casserole tightly and simmer over low heat for 1 hour. Uncover, turn the meat over, cover, and continue to cook for 45 to 50 minutes, until very tender. Remove the meat to a platter.

Reduce the sauce over high heat, breaking up the tomatoes a little with a wooden spoon. Cook until the juices thicken substantially, then add salt and pepper to taste. Pour over the osso buco and serve.

Serves 4

Grilled Veal Chop, Yellow Tomato Coulis, and Basil Oil

About a decade ago, scaloppine were displaced by grilled chops as the most trendy and desirable cut of veal. A satisfying dish that bridges the seasons, the veal chop is equally delicious with red tomato coulis when yellow ones are unavailable.

> 4 rib veal chops, each 1¼ inches thick
>
> Basil Oil (page 156), warmed
>
> Yellow Tomato Coulis (page 156), warmed

Preheat the oven to 350°.

Season the veal chops with salt and freshly ground black pepper. Brush lightly with some of the basil oil.

In a well-seasoned cast-iron skillet, sear the veal chops on both sides until browned. Finish cooking in the oven until done, about 15 minutes.

Divide the tomato coulis evenly on the plates. Top with the veal chops and spoon more basil oil over the top.

Serves 4

ADD-ONS

Garnish with fresh basil and Slow-Roasted Romas (page 220).

GRAPENOTE

A luscious red Italian wine with a touch of berry fruit makes a special partner for this dish. Try a Rosso di Montalcino. Want something French? Open a Rully Rouge, medium-bodied with a true Burgundian bouquet.

Yellow Tomato Coulis

12 ounces large yellow tomatoes, blanched and peeled
1 tablespoon extra-virgin olive oil

Cut the tomatoes in half and squeeze out the seeds. Cut in large pieces. Place the tomatoes in a blender, add the oil, and puree until smooth. Add salt and pepper to taste.

Makes ¾ cup

Basil Oil

1 large bunch fresh basil
6 tablespoons extra-virgin olive oil

Remove the leaves from the stems and wash. Blanch the leaves in boiling water for 1 minute. Plunge in ice water. Drain and gently squeeze the water from the basil. Place in a blender. Add oil and puree until smooth. Add salt to taste. Refrigerate.

Makes ⅔ cup

Arista: Roast Pork Loin with Rosemary and Garlic

I was nineteen, in Siena, and in love with Italy when I tasted my first arista; nothing has erased the memory of this triumphant marriage of ingredients. Have it with a glass of Chianti, as I did. Kiss your butcher, and ask him to saw through the bones for easy carving.

3½- to 4-pound loin of pork, bones trimmed
    but not removed

3 tablespoons fresh rosemary leaves, minced

2 tablespoons finely chopped fresh garlic

Pat the pork loin dry with paper towels. In a mortar and pestle, or with a fork and wooden board, make a coarse paste of the rosemary, the garlic, ½ teaspoon kosher salt, and ½ teaspoon butcher-grind black pepper. Spread all over the pork loin and let stand for 1 hour.

Preheat the oven to 325°.

Roast for 1½ hours (about 25 minutes per pound) or until a meat thermometer reads 155°. Let meat rest while making the sauce.

Add boiling water and 1 to 2 teaspoons freshly chopped rosemary leaves to the pan juices. Slice the pork and serve with the pan juices.

ADD-ONS

You can deglaze the pan with white wine, if desired. Serve with Broccoli di Rape with Anchovies and Pignoli (page 196). To serve cold: Slice thin and cover with a veil of Anchovy-Lemon Mayonnaise (page 139).

GRAPENOTES

Try a geographically correct Chianti Classico to accompany this fragrant pork roast.

Barbecued Pork Pull

This is a pungent, mouthwatering dish that triggers ISR (instant salivary response). It sticks not only to your ribs but also to your pot, so cook it in Teflon for easy cleanup. Serve with Cheddar-Pepper Grits (page 199) and let the good times roll.

(page 199)

1 pork shoulder roast, about 6 pounds

1½ cups cider vinegar

1 cup ketchup

Preheat the oven to 300°.

Brown the roast in a large nonstick skillet and then place it in a Dutch oven. Mix the cider vinegar, the ketchup, 2 cups water, 2 teaspoons salt, and lots of freshly ground black pepper in a saucepan and bring to a boil. Pour it over the roast and cover.

Bake 40 minutes to the pound, basting occasionally with drippings. Turn once every hour. The meat should be very soft when done.

Transfer the roast to a chopping board. Remove the meat from the bone and chop it into fairly fine pieces. Add any solids from the cooking liquid to the meat. Season to taste with additional vinegar, salt, and pepper.

Makes 2¼ pounds, serving 6

ADD-ONS

Serve with your own "Condiment Bar": Put an assortment of hot sauces on a tray and pass to your guests. Serve with good-quality white bread or freshly made Beer Bread (page 101).

GRAPENOTE

Have a beer . . . or two.

Pork Chops with Vinegar Peppers

Peperoncini, a sprightly Italian condiment of little green hot peppers in a vinegary brine, makes a mouthwatering foil for thick, meaty pork chops. Sauté the chops slowly for optimum moistness. This will surely become a family favorite.

> 1 cup peperoncini, drained
>
> 4 thick pork chops, 5 to 6 ounces each
>
> 4½ tablespoons good-quality olive oil

Drain the jar of peperoncini. Pick out the smallest peppers to use.

Dust the pork chops with salt and freshly ground black pepper. Heat 1 tablespoon of the olive oil in a large nonstick skillet. Sauté the chops on each side until cooked to the desired degree of doneness, being careful not to overcook. Remove from the pan and keep warm.

Add 3½ tablespoons olive oil to the pan, scraping up any browned bits. Add the peppers and sauté for 3 to 4 minutes, until soft. Pour the peppers and the oil over the pork chops. Serve immediately.

Serves 4

ADD-ONS

Add 2 cloves of thinly sliced garlic to the pan with the peppers. Serve with hot, crusty Italian bread.

GRAPENOTE

Two different styles of wine will satisfy in very different ways. Try a bold chilled Lindemans Semillon-Chardonnay with a touch of sweetness to complement hot and spicy flavors. Or try an inky red wine equal to the considerable heft of the dish—such as Salice Salentino, from southern Italy.

Roast Pork Tenderloin
with Prunes and Bay Leaves

GRAPENOTE

Try the suggestions in the headnote: a chardonnay or Beaujolais, depending on your choice of accompaniments.

In France, where the mention of prunes never causes a snicker, this dish would have a distinct bistro feel. Try with Hubbard Squash and Orange Puree (page 179) and a chardonnay. For a different style, have it with Caramelized Endive and Bacon (page 176) and a glass of Beaujolais.

8 California bay leaves

15 large pitted prunes

1½ pounds pork tenderloin

Place the bay leaves and prunes in a bowl. Pour 1½ cups boiling water over the top and let sit 15 minutes.

Preheat the oven to 400°.

Make a 1-inch-deep slit along the length of the tenderloin, leaving 1 inch uncut on each end.

Remove the bay leaves and prunes from the water and pat dry with paper towels. Place the prunes in the bottom of the slit in a tight row. Crumble 1 bay leaf finely and sprinkle it over the prunes.

Roll the meat and tie it tightly at 1-inch intervals. Sprinkle with salt and pepper on all sides. Place the remaining bay leaves under the strings.

Spray a baking pan with vegetable-oil cooking spray and place the tenderloin in the pan. Roast for 30 to 35 minutes. Let rest 5 minutes before slicing. Remove the bay leaves.

Serves 4

Garlic Sausage, Lentils, and Diced Carrots

French garlic sausage or Italian cotechino are required for this robust country dish—its ingredients belong to both countries. These styles of sausages are made with the fattier parts of the pig and need to be cooked. You can buy great garlic sausage from D'Artagnan (see Sources, page 291), or ask your Italian butcher for cotechino.

1½ pounds garlic sausage or cotechino sausage

12 ounces lentils

3 large carrots, peeled

Put the sausage in a large pot and cover with 8 cups cold water. Bring to a boil, lower the heat, and simmer 45 minutes. Remove the sausage and set aside.

Wash the lentils, drain, and add to the sausage cooking liquid. Bring to a boil. Add ½ teaspoon whole black peppercorns, lower the heat, and cook the lentils 35 to 40 minutes, until they are soft but not falling apart. Drain and keep warm.

Meanwhile, dice the carrots into ⅛-inch cubes. Boil in a small amount of salted water for 8 minutes, or until soft. Drain and keep warm.

When ready to serve, boil the sausage in water for 2 minutes to reheat. Place the warm lentils on a platter. Cut the sausage into 1-inch-thick slices and place on top. Scatter the carrots over the sausage and lentils. Serve immediately.

Serves 4

ADD-ONS

A few leaves of fried sage would be nice, as would a small pot of Dijon mustard.

GRAPENOTES

French? Serve full-bodied Beaujolais. Italian? Drink Nebbiolo. New Year's Eve? Drink champagne.

Calf's Liver with Home-Dried Grapes

ADD-ONS

Add 2 tablespoons brandy to the pan juices and grapes. Cook 1 minute over high heat to let alcohol evaporate. Garnish with fresh chervil.

GRAPENOTE

Relish with a graceful California pinot noir or elegant French red Burgundy.

Not a liver lover? You won't be able to resist these rosy, thin slices of tender meat punctuated with bursts of sweet grape flavor. Grapes prepared in this manner are halfway down the road to raisins but are more voluptuous. Serve with Gratin Dauphinoise (page 192) for a memorable meal.

1 pound red and green seedless grapes (or just green seedless)

1 pound calf's liver, in one piece

2 tablespoons unsalted butter

Preheat the oven to 400°.

Place the grapes on a baking sheet and roast for 25 minutes, shaking the pan several times during roasting to prevent sticking. Reduce the oven temperature to 275°. Bake an additional 40 minutes. Remove from the oven and reserve.

Sprinkle the liver with salt and freshly ground black pepper. In a nonstick skillet, melt 1 tablespoon butter. When it starts to brown, add the liver and sauté on both sides until the liver begins to crisp on the outside but is still pinkish on the inside.

Add the reserved grapes and cook 1 or 2 minutes. Remove the liver to a warm platter, leaving the grapes in the pan. Add 1 tablespoon butter to the pan with a few tablespoons boiling water and heat sauce 1 minute over high heat, scraping any browned bits off the bottom of the pan. Slice the liver on the bias and pour the sauce over the top.

Serves 4

Lamb Shanks Alsatian-Style

Inspired by a dish at Restaurant JoJo, in New York, I created a version of Alsatian "baeckeofe," or "baker's oven," using my favorite hunk of meat: a lamb shank. Make sure your enamel-glazed casserole has a secure cover, as you want the shanks to bathe in their winy onion sauce.

> **2 large lamb shanks, 1½ pounds each**
>
> **1¼ pounds yellow onions**
>
> **2 cups dry Alsatian riesling**

Preheat the broiler.

Salt and pepper the lamb shanks and place them on a baking sheet. Broil 5 minutes on each side. Remove from the broiler. Lower the heat to 350°. Peel the onions and slice them in half lengthwise, then across into ¼-inch-thick slices. Put in the bottom of a heavy shallow casserole (an enamel Le Creuset is best).

Place the shanks on the onions. Cover and bake 1 hour. Turn shanks and add 1½ cups wine. Cover and bake 1 hour longer.

Remove the shanks with tongs to a warm platter. Place the casserole on top of the stove. Add ½ cup white wine and salt and pepper to taste. Cook over medium-high heat, scraping up any browned bits, for 2 minutes to finish sauce. Pour over the lamb shanks.

Serves 2

ADD-ONS

Serve with French Potato Cake (page 207).

GRAPENOTE

Continue to drink the good-quality wine you used in cooking this dish, or go up the flavor scale a bit and serve Pinot Auxerrois, also from Alsace.

Lamb Steaks with Tomatoes and Za'atar

One bite will transport you to the land of the Pharaohs, where lamb is king of the meal. A sauce of za'atar and tomatoes lends an unfamiliar yet haunting flavor to a juicy lamb steak cut from the leg. You can substitute shoulder chops, but they won't be as tender.

1 (28-ounce) can plum tomatoes in puree

2 tablespoons za'atar spice (see Sources, page 289)

6 lamb steaks or shoulder chops, 8 ounces each

Put the tomatoes and puree in a medium-size heavy pot and cook slowly over low heat for 20 minutes, mashing lightly with a spoon or potato masher. Add za'atar and cook 10 minutes longer; the sauce will become thick. Reserve. Makes 2 cups.

Season the lamb with salt and freshly ground pepper. In a large nonstick skillet, sear the lamb on both sides until crisp and rare. Add the sauce and heat 5 minutes.

Serves 6

ADD-ONS

Add crumbled feta cheese to the top of the sauce and bake in the oven at 400° for 2 to 3 minutes. Serve with basmati rice.

GRAPENOTE

Now's the time for a blockbuster merlot from California. Or go Med-Rim with a merlot from Yarden Winery in Israel's Golan Heights or a Château Musar red wine from Lebanon.

Rack of Lamb with Pesto Crumbs

Definitely a dish for a VIP. Choose a rack from a young lamb and have your butcher "french" the ends of the bones by scraping them clean just up to the eye of the meat. You can use a good-quality prepared pesto, or if you can handle a few more ingredients, make your own. Fresh bread crumbs are a must. Honor your guest with a glass of mouth-filling Côtes Rôtie or Shiraz from Australia.

1½-pound rack of lamb, trimmed, flap removed, bones exposed (8 ribs)

⅓ cup pesto sauce—plus more for serving if desired

¾ cup bread crumbs made from fresh bread

Preheat the oven to 375°.

Season the lamb with salt and freshly ground black pepper. Spread the pesto sauce over the surface of the meat.

Coat the meat thoroughly with bread crumbs. Cover the bones with aluminum foil and place the lamb on a baking sheet. Roast for 15 minutes, remove the foil, and bake 20 minutes longer. Remove from the oven, let rest 5 minutes, and carve, slicing into thick double chops or single chops. Serve with additional pesto sauce if desired.

Serves 2 to 4

GRAPENOTE

Spend some money for a great Côtes Rôtie, such as Domaine de Bonserine from France; or drink Penfolds Bin 389 cabernet-shiraz from Australia, or Sequoia Grove merlot from California.

Turkish Lamb Chops

Worthy of a sultan, this authentic preparation of thick loin chops typifies the sensational grilled meats of the eastern Mediterranean. If an outdoor grill is not handy, sear in a cast-iron grill pan or broil close to the source of heat. Nice with a squeeze of fresh lemon and a helping of Turkish Pilaf with Tomato.

2 large onions, grated

⅓ cup extra-virgin olive oil

12 loin lamb chops, 1 inch thick

Sprinkle the grated onions with 1 teaspoon salt. Squeeze out the juice of the onions and discard. Mix the onions with the oil. Brush the lamb chops on both sides with this marinade, and let stand for 1 hour.

Grill the chops, preferably over charcoal, on both sides. Sprinkle with salt and lots of cracked black pepper.

Serves 4

ADD-ONS

Place 2 tablespoons fresh thyme leaves in the marinade. Serve the lamb chops with wedges of fresh lemon, fried potatoes, or authentic Turkish Pilaf with Tomato (page 180).

GRAPENOTE

Serve with a robust merlot from Hargrave Vineyard, on Long Island, or a white with strong character, such as Greco di Tufo, from southern Italy, or even a white retsina from Greece.

Maple-Glazed Corned Beef

A blustery March day, when the sap of mighty maples has started to rise, seems a good time to make this dish and celebrate St. Patrick's Day in a New England fashion. Only the aromatic flavor of real maple syrup will do.

4 to 5 pounds corned beef

30 whole cloves

½ cup pure maple syrup

In an enameled casserole, cover the corned beef with water and bring to a boil. Lower the heat, cover, and simmer until done, allowing 50 to 55 minutes per pound. Place on a rack in an open roasting pan. Stick with whole cloves in a cross-hatch design.

Preheat the oven to 375°.

Pour the syrup over the meat and put in the oven to brown and glaze for about 15 minutes. Baste occasionally with syrup.

Serves 6 to 8

ADD-ONS

Serve with Chardonnay Cabbage (page 198) and boiled fingerling or new potatoes.

GRAPENOTE

You need a wine with a bit of sweetness: a California chenin blanc or a rosé like Heitz's Grignolino.

Coffee and Vinegar Pot Roast

I've collected over the years a stack of wacky and wonderful recipes from a variety of odd sources. Many come from community cooks, who are never shy about displaying naiveté. My favorite, originally known as Lutheran Ladies Peking Beef Roast, says to "burn on both sides and douse with coffee." Improbable perhaps, but delicious.

5-pound chuck roast or bottom round

1 cup white wine vinegar

2 cups strong, hot black coffee

Put the meat in a large, nonmetallic bowl and pour the vinegar over it. Refrigerate 24 to 48 hours, turning several times.

Remove the meat from the marinade, reserving the vinegar. Pat the meat dry with paper towels and brown it in a heavy pot until nearly burned on both sides. The meat will generate its own fat.

Pour the coffee and 1 cup water over the roast and scrape up the browned bits with a wooden spoon. Add 2 tablespoons whole black peppercorns (or a combination of black and white) and ½ tablespoon salt. Cover and cook slowly for 3½ hours, or until fork-tender. Turn several times during cooking. Remove the meat and keep warm.

Add the reserved vinegar if desired, add salt and pepper to taste, and reduce the liquid until you have 3 cups. Thinly slice the meat and heat in the gravy for ½ hour longer over very low heat.

Serves 6 to 8

ADD-ONS

Add 2 bay leaves to the cooking liquid. Serve with Turnip and Havarti Torte (page 177), Potato-Fennel Mash (page 190), or French Potato Cake (page 207).

GRAPENOTE

Try any one of the younger "cabs" from California or experiment with one of the new Meritage blends of cabernet, merlot, and cabernet franc.

Steak Haché, Cabernet Butter

Pretty fancy name for a hamburger, but this "chopped steak" does taste fancy under a blanket of buttery red wine sauce known as "beurre rouge." Serve with the veg du jour: Whole Roasted Garlic with Goat Cheese (page 184). Go ahead and finish that bottle of cab.

1¼ pounds chopped sirloin

3 tablespoons unsalted butter, cold

½ cup cabernet sauvignon

Divide the sirloin into two equal portions. Mold into large oval shapes, to look something like a steak. Season with salt and freshly ground black pepper.

In a large nonstick skillet, melt ½ tablespoon of the butter. Add the meat and sear on each side 3 to 4 minutes, so that the outside is well browned and the inside is rare to medium-rare.

Remove the "steaks" to platter. Add the wine to the pan and reduce over high heat. Add ½ teaspoon butcher-grind black pepper and salt to taste. When reduced by half, remove from the heat and whisk in the remaining cold butter. Pour the sauce over the "steaks." Serve immediately.

Serves 2

ADD-ONS

Add 1 tablespoon drained green peppercorns to the sauce instead of black pepper.

GRAPENOTE

Open a bottle of your favorite cabernet sauvignon, a not-too-expensive Bordeaux, or a Spanish red Rioja.

Pan-Seared Sirloin, Oyster Sauce Reduction

ADD-ONS

Garnish with fresh
chopped chives. To
serve Carpetbag-style,
top with plump
poached oysters.

GRAPENOTE

White wine with
meat? Try a
blockbuster barrel-
fermented
chardonnay from
California or
Australia. If you
believe in red, try a
bodacious Cornas
or Amarone.

*If there were such a thing as a Chinese steakhouse, this is the sort of dish
it would serve—strong in flavor and suave in texture. As a twist on the
classic Carpetbag Steak, which is steak and oysters, top with several of
the plump juicy bivalves, poached briefly in simmering water.*

4 New York cut strip steaks, 12 ounces each

3½ tablespoons unsalted butter, cold

3 tablespoons Chinese oyster sauce

On a clean kitchen towel, crack 4 teaspoons white peppercorns with
a hammer or the flat side of a cleaver. Press the cracked peppercorns
into the top of each steak, pounding lightly with your fist.

Melt ½ tablespoon of the butter in a large nonstick skillet. Cook
the steaks over high heat on each side until lightly caramelized. Remove the steaks and keep warm.

Add the oyster sauce to the pan. Bring to a boil. Remove from the
heat and whisk in the remaining butter, cut into small pieces. The
sauce will get creamy.

Slice the steaks thickly on the bias, or leave whole. Pour the sauce
over the top.

Serves 4

Mahogany Short Ribs

This irreverent merger of foodstuffs results in a tantalizing dish that will amaze and amuse your guests. Prune juice tenderizes marbled ribs of beef, while teriyaki sauce adds a touch of sweetness and salinity. Nice with a bright, young zinfandel.

> 3 pounds short ribs, cut into 4 pieces (see Note)
>
> 1 cup teriyaki sauce
>
> 1 cup prune juice

Cover the meat in a mixture of teriyaki sauce and prune juice. Refrigerate, covered, overnight.

Remove the ribs from the marinade. Bring the marinade to a boil in a large pot with 1 cup water and ½ teaspoon whole black peppercorns. Lower the heat, add the meat, and cover. Simmer for 2 hours, or until meat is very tender.

Remove the ribs to a platter. Reduce the sauce for 5 minutes or until syrupy over medium-high heat. Pour it over short ribs.

This is also delicious the next day. Remove any congealed fat from the top of the sauce and slowly reheat the ribs in the liquid.

Serves 4

ADD-ONS

Serve with freshly cooked broad Egg Noodles with Butter and Rosemary (page 214). Top with a mound of steamed haricots verts for drama.

GRAPENOTE

Uncork a bottle of California zinfandel and let it "open" in the glass before serving the main course. Its rich berry taste and long finish will balance the sweetness and salinity in this dish. Look for zins that are labeled "old vines" for the most concentrated fruit.

Note: Have the butcher cut the short ribs between the bones into 4 pieces. These are known as "long cut" to differentiate them from "flanken." Trim off the outer flap.

Fillet of Beef, Gorgonzola Whipped Potatoes

This sounds like a he-man recipe, but the result is really a sophisticated dish for company. The meat is at its best when rare. Serve with a special-occasion cabernet or French Bordeaux.

> 1½ pounds all-purpose potatoes
>
> 6 ounces Italian Gorgonzola, Cambazola, or Blue Castello cheese
>
> 2½ pounds fillet of beef

Peel the potatoes and cut into quarters. Place in a pot with salted water to cover. Bring to a boil, lower heat, and simmer 30 to 40 minutes, until soft. With a slotted spoon, transfer the potatoes to the bowl of electric mixer. Reserve ½ cup of the cooking liquid. Cut the cheese into small pieces and add it to the potatoes. Whip until light and fluffy. Add a little cooking liquid if necessary. Add salt and pepper.

Preheat the oven to 400°.

Season the fillet with salt and pepper. Put on a baking sheet and roast 25 to 30 minutes, until the meat reaches an internal temperature of 130°. Remove from oven and let rest 10 minutes.

Warm the potatoes in a heavy pot over low heat, stirring often. Spoon the potatoes into the center of 6 large, warm dinner plates. Carve the fillet into 1½-inch-thick slices. Put a slice on top of each mound of potatoes. Spoon any pan juices over the meat.

Serves 6

Hot Tip: To make mashed potato soup, add 1 cup potato cooking liquid to potato-cheese mixture. Bring to a boil. Pass through a coarse sieve. Serve hot. Makes 2½ cups.

ADD-ONS

Serve with Melted Tomatoes (page 221) or French Beans with Toasted Hazelnuts (page 182)

GRAPENOTE

Lots of wonderful possibilities: try Chateau Gloria; a warm lusty red from the Côtes du Roussillon; a Spanish Tempranillo from Ribera del Duero, or a California cab from Mondavi.

Prime Ribs of Beef, Horseradish-Rye Crust

As families have gotten smaller, we've forgotten the domestic pleasure of home-roasted prime ribs of beef. The twist here lies in the pungency of horseradish that is punched up by the flavor of caraway.

> 6 to 7 pounds standing ribs of beef, tied (3 or 4 ribs), at room temperature
>
> 6 tablespoons prepared white horseradish
>
> 8 slices rye bread with caraway seeds, made into bread crumbs

Preheat oven to 300°.

Place the meat on a rack in a roasting pan and put it in the oven. Remove roast from oven after 90 minutes. Increase the oven temperature to 400°. Carefully drain any fat and juices from the pan and reserve. Coat the exterior of the roast with horseradish. Cover evenly with bread crumbs, packing it down with your hands. Sprinkle with salt and freshly ground black pepper. Drizzle the pan juices over the crumbs.

Return the roast to the oven. Finish cooking until desired doneness is reached, about 30 minutes. A meat thermometer should read 135° to 140° for rare, 145° to 150° for medium rare.

Serves 6 to 8

ADD-ONS

Serve with Turnip and Havarti Torte (page 177) and Sugar Snaps in Orange Butter (page 191).

GRAPENOTE

Try a bottle of voluptuous Bonny Doon Syrah; Cahors from the Dordogne, or the Hungarian Egri Bikaver, affectionately known as "bull's blood."

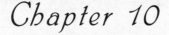

Chapter 10

Vegetables and
Side Dishes

*S*exy and inexpensive, side dishes are stealing the show in all the best restaurants. Why not at home?

Today the accent is on intriguing and unexpected starches—the mashed potato has been elevated to celebrity status—and vegetable accompaniments are designed to knock your socks off.

Bulghur and barley, couscous and polenta, grits and rice, even the humble bean carry flavors easily and have a comforting feel in the mouth. They mold into interesting shapes and are delicious at a variety of temperatures.

Best of all, my three-ingredient vegetables and side dishes have high flavor profiles and assertive textures; in combination, they constitute terrific meatless meals.

Caramelized Endive and Bacon

The torpedoes of slender white leaves that we know as Belgian endive are usually used in salad. But this braised dish—a fascinating balance of bitter, sweet, salt, and smoke—is handsome enough to serve by itself as a first course or an indulgent side dish.

4 medium or large heads Belgian endive

8 slices bacon

2 tablespoons balsamic vinegar

Preheat the oven to 400°.

Remove any dark or bruised outer leaves. Wrap 2 slices of bacon around each endive in a spiral and secure with wooden toothpicks. Place the endive in a shallow baking dish with ¼ cup water. Bake for 40 minutes. Sprinkle each endive with ½ tablespoon vinegar, turn, and bake 10 minutes longer.

Remove from the oven. Sprinkle with additional balsamic vinegar and freshly ground black pepper. Serve hot as a side dish or at room temperature as a first course.

Serves 4

Turnip and Havarti Torte

My simplified adaptation of a medieval recipe turns a much-reviled root vegetable into a refined accompaniment that looks surprisingly like a cake. It's a delicious foil for full-flavored or fatty meats like duck and pork—I even love it cold. Use large white turnips for the prettiest results.

> 2½ pounds large white turnips
>
> 2 tablespoons unsalted butter, at room temperature
>
> 1 pound caraway havarti cheese, in 1/16-inch slices

Boil the unpeeled turnips in salted water for 30 minutes or until tender. Drain, cool, peel, and cut into ¼-inch-thick slices. Pat dry with paper towels.

Preheat the oven to 375°.

Spread the butter in the bottom of a 9-inch springform pan. Arrange layer of cheese on bottom, using one-fourth of the cheese. Add a layer of turnip slices (overlapping slightly) and sprinkle very lightly with salt and freshly ground pepper. Continue layering (another two layers), ending with a layer of cheese on top. Place pan on baking sheet.

Bake 40 minutes. When finished, the cheese should be golden brown. Let cool slightly before serving. Remove from the pan. Cut into wedges.

This is even better the next day when reheated.

Serves 10 to 12

Fried Lemon and Zucchini Salad

This may be my favorite edible invention. A wake-up call to your taste buds, this dish adds syncopated bursts of Mediterranean flavor to fish, veal, and lamb. If there's any left over, try it instead of mundane tomato in a sandwich.

1 pound medium zucchini

Olive oil, about ⅓ cup

2 large thin-skinned lemons

Wash the zucchini. Slice on a bias, about ⅓ inch thick. Sprinkle with 1 teaspoon salt and place in colander. Let stand 1 hour. Rinse well and dry thoroughly.

In a medium-size skillet, fry small batches quickly in hot shallow oil, turning once, until golden brown. Drain on paper towels and place in a bowl.

Slice the lemons very thin. Add to the hot oil and fry, turning once. The lemons will brown and the oil will thicken into a delicious sauce. Add the cooked lemons to the zucchini and add some of the lemon oil. Let marinate one hour at room temperature before serving. Sprinkle with salt and freshly ground black pepper.

Serves 4

ADD-ONS

You can add 1 teaspoon freshly minced garlic to the bowl while marinating, or 1 tablespoon finely chopped mint.

GREAT IDEA

Serve with freshly grilled or steamed halibut or red snapper. Also delicious alongside grilled lamb kebabs.

Hubbard Squash and Orange Puree

Forget all those watery squashes that ruined Aunt Maud's dinners! This is an intense, perfumed recipe that adds great interest (and a brilliant orange color) to simple roast birds and meats. If you can't find Hubbard squash, use another winter squash, like butternut or acorn.

2 pounds Hubbard squash

1 orange

2 tablespoons unsalted butter

Preheat the oven to 400°.

Cut the squash in half lengthwise, then in half crosswise. Remove seeds and any membrane. Place in baking pan flesh side down and pour ¼ cup water over the top. Bake for 1 hour, turning over after 30 minutes. Squash will be lightly caramelized.

Remove the flesh from the skin, put it in a food processor, and puree until smooth. Add 2 teaspoons freshly grated orange zest and 2 tablespoons fresh orange juice. Cut the butter into small pieces and add it to the processor. Process again. Add salt and pepper to taste.

Makes 2 cups, serving 4 to 5

Turkish Pilaf with Tomato

"Handkerchief steaming" is what makes this dish authentically Turkish. It is a great pilaf, the texture tantamount to perfection.

1 cup long-grain rice or basmati rice

1 tablespoon unsalted butter

2 cups tomato juice

Place the rice in a bowl with 2 teaspoons salt. Pour boiling water over, stir, and let stand until water cools. Drain the rice, wash it well under cold water, and drain again. Set aside.

Place the butter, the tomato juice, and 1 teaspoon salt in a heavy saucepan and bring to a boil. Add the rice, stir, cover, and boil over high heat for 2 minutes. Lower heat and cook slowly until the rice absorbs all the liquid.

Turn off the heat, uncover, place a clean handkerchief or kitchen towel over the saucepan, replace the cover, and let the pilaf stand for 30 minutes before serving. A wooden spoon is recommended to transfer pilaf from saucepan to serving plate.

Serves 4

ADD-ONS

Put a small cinnamon stick in the water when boiling the rice. Remove before serving.

Watercress Puree
("Tastes Like Creamed Spinach")

Small, peppery watercress is overlooked as a vegetable. When cooked, it makes an AstroTurf-green puree that will rival the best creamed spinach. Spoon into a large, hot baked potato for a great supper.

> 12 ounces boiling potatoes
>
> 1 pound watercress (4 large bunches), washed well
>
> 3 tablespoons unsalted butter, cold, cut into several pieces

Bring 8 cups of water plus 1½ teaspoons salt to a boil. Peel potatoes. Slice in half lengthwise, then across into ½-inch slices. Place in boiling water, lower heat to medium, and cook 20 minutes.

Trim 1½ inches off stems of watercress and discard. Add watercress to potatoes after 20 minutes and cook 10 minutes longer.

Drain. Transfer potatoes and watercress to food processor. Puree until thick and smooth, slowly adding the cold butter. Return to the heat and warm before serving. Add salt to taste (don't add pepper).

Makes 2 cups, serving 4 to 5

ADD-ONS

A little freshly grated nutmeg brings out the flavor.

French Beans with Toasted Hazelnuts

Years ago, if you had a pile of thin, tiny string beans on your plate, you were either in Paris or in a French restaurant. Luckily, haricots verts are available today in many well-stocked produce markets and are particularly glamorous when tossed with bits of toasted hazelnuts.

ADD-ONS

Sprinkle the beans with 1 teaspoon tarragon vinegar while sautéing.

1 pound haricots verts, trimmed (or string beans trimmed and julienned lengthwise)

⅓ cup coarsely chopped hazelnuts, lightly toasted

3 tablespoons unsalted butter

Bring salted water to a boil. Add the green beans and blanch 5 minutes. Quickly shock in a colander under cold water. Drain well.

Just before serving, sauté the hazelnuts in the butter. Add the green beans and, tossing lightly, heat until they are warm. Add salt and pepper to taste.

Serves 4 to 6

Zucchini, Black Olive, and Tomato Compote

Move over, ratatouille; this triptych of Mediterranean flavors is as memorable, and much easier to prepare. A wonderful, jamlike accompaniment to grilled tuna or juicy medallions of veal, it is also great on a baguette with sliced hard-boiled eggs.

1¼ cups crushed tomatoes in puree

12 ounces small zucchini

18 oil-cured black olives, pitted

In a large nonstick skillet, heat the crushed tomatoes for 5 minutes over medium heat until slightly reduced.

Wash the zucchini and pat it dry. Slice into ½-inch-thick circles. Add it to the tomatoes and cook for 15 to 20 minutes, or until the zucchini becomes soft and translucent. Add a few tablespoons of water if sauce is too thick. Add olives, ¼ teaspoon salt, and lots of freshly ground black pepper. Continue to cook 2 to 3 minutes.

Let cool and serve at room temperature.

Makes 2 cups, serving 4

ADD-ONS

Drizzle with a flavored olive oil. Add several strips of fresh orange zest to tomatoes.

Whole Roasted Garlic with Goat Cheese

ADD-ONS

Serve with mixed greens tossed with Lemon Vinaigrette (page 56) as a memorable salad course for company.

However unthinkable it may be to eat a head of garlic, this is so delicious it would be more unthinkable not to. The pulp becomes soft and spreadable and transfixingly mild. Serve with a crusty baguette.

4 whole large heads garlic

¼ cup aromatic olive oil

2 ounces fresh goat cheese in a log

Preheat the oven to 300°.

Cut ⅓ inch off the top of the heads of garlic. Put the garlic in a small baking dish with 3 tablespoons water. Sprinkle with 1 teaspoon coarse salt and drizzle oil over the tops of the garlic.

Bake, basting often, for 1¼ hours, or until the garlic cloves are very soft (many restaurants that serve this dish do not bake the garlic long enough).

Top each head with ½-ounce slice of goat cheese and broil 1 minute, or until golden.

Serves 4

Rosemary-Roasted Potatoes

Cut in large wedges or homey chunks, these potatoes are designed to please. Long baking gives them an appealing crust enveloping a creamy interior. And rosemary is a potato's best friend.

8 medium potatoes (about 2 pounds)

3½ tablespoons chopped fresh rosemary (see Note)

¼ cup extra-virgin olive oil

Preheat the oven to 400°.

Peel the potatoes and cut them into 4 to 6 chunks or long wedges.

In a large bowl, make a paste of 3 tablespoons of the rosemary, the olive oil, and 1½ teaspoons coarse salt. Add the potatoes and evenly coat them with the mixture, adding a little more oil if needed.

Place in a baking dish and bake 40 to 45 minutes, until browned, turning occasionally with a spatula.

Sprinkle with ½ tablespoon coarsely chopped fresh rosemary and additional coarse salt.

Serves 4 to 6

Note: You can substitute 2 teaspooons crumbled dried rosemary.

Smothered Lettuce with Sumac

You hardly ever come across cooked lettuce, but when gently sautéed with salty-sour sumac, iceberg yields its moisture and softens gracefully. This is a beguiling accompaniment to chicken and lamb, and even your foodie friends won't guess what it is.

ADD-ONS

Serve at room temperature with hot Med-Rim Lamb Nuggets (page 45), or as an unusual first course.

1 pound iceberg lettuce

3 tablespoons extra-virgin olive oil

1 tablespoon ground sumac (see Note)

Wash the lettuce, coarsely chop it, and put it in a bowl with the olive oil. Mix well. Add sumac and toss.

Heat a large nonstick skillet and put the lettuce mixture in the hot skillet. Cook over medium-high heat 10 minutes, or until lettuce is wilted and dark green in color. Drizzle with extra olive oil if desired. Add a pinch of salt and pepper. Serve hot or cold.

Serves 3 to 4

Note: Sumac is the small red berries of a shrub originating in Turkey, dried and ground into a powder that has a lemony, salty taste. Available in Middle Eastern food stores (see Sources, page 289).

Steamed Broccoli, Stir-Fried Pecans

It's hard to believe that three simple ingredients can pack such a flavor wallop. This is one time you don't want your broccoli al dente but slightly soft to contrast better with the crunch of pecans. Definitely a crowd-pleasing, East-meets-West veggie.

1 large bunch broccoli

⅓ cup coarsely chopped pecans

2 tablespoons Chinese oyster sauce

Cut the broccoli into large florets, leaving 1½ inches of stem. You should have 1 pound florets (save the rest of the stems for another use). Steam the broccoli florets over boiling water for 8 to 10 minutes. They should be starting to soften but should still be bright green.

Meanwhile, toast the pecans in a nonstick skillet until they become dark brown, being careful not to let them burn.

In a large bowl, toss the hot steamed broccoli, the toasted pecans, and the oyster sauce. Season to taste with sea salt and freshly ground black pepper. Serve immediately.

Serves 4

Spoonbread Custard

A "fallen soufflé" with a dense, creamy center, this dish speaks of elegant Southern hospitality. Serve it hot with cold buttermilk poured on top and pass the pepper mill. Or serve alongside Mesclun and Blood Orange Salad (page 75) for a lovely lunch.

1 cup yellow cornmeal

4 extra-large eggs, separated

1 cup buttermilk

Preheat the oven to 400°.

Put the cornmeal in a bowl and add 1 cup cold water. Put another cup of water in a saucepan with 1 teaspoon salt and bring to a boil. Stir in the wet cornmeal and cook 1 minute, stirring constantly with a wooden spoon. Remove from the heat. Add egg yolks, buttermilk, and freshly ground black pepper and mix well.

Beat the egg whites with a pinch of salt until thick. Fold into the cornmeal mixture.

Lightly coat a casserole with vegetable spray and pour the cornmeal mixture into the casserole. Bake 35 to 40 minutes, until golden brown and puffy. Serve hot with additional cold buttermilk poured on top.

Serves 6 to 8

White Polenta with Parmigiano-Reggiano

Polenta is usually made by adding cornmeal in a slow, steady stream to a pot of boiling water. Instead, when preparing white polenta, I add cold water to the cornmeal as a better way of reducing lumps. The result: white-on-white, ultra-creamy richness.

1½ cups white cornmeal

1 small clove garlic, pushed through a garlic press

7 tablespoons grated Parmigiano-Reggiano cheese

Place the cornmeal and 1 teaspoon salt in a large saucepan. Gradually add 5 cups water and then the garlic, stirring constantly with a wooden spoon to remove any lumps. Bring to a boil, reduce the heat to medium, and cook, uncovered, about 10 minutes. Add 5 tablespoons grated cheese and continue cooking and stirring frequently for 5 minutes more.

Spread the polenta on a heatproof platter, sprinkle with the remaining cheese, and broil 1 minute.

Makes 4 cups, serving 6 to 8

ADD-ONS

This is an interesting side dish when ¾ cup cooked tiny frozen peas (petits pois) are added. As a first course, top with Grilled Shiitake Mushrooms, Garlic Essence (page 76). For "matzoh polenta," substitute matzoh meal for cornmeal.

Potato-Fennel Mash

ADD-ONS

If you want a creamier consistency, add more butter or 2 or 3 table-spoons heavy cream.

An old-fashioned potato ricer is what gives this potato dish its special consistency. Fennel gives it a special taste. Decorate with feathery fennel fronds.

1½ pounds potatoes

12 ounces fennel bulb, with fronds

2½ tablespoons unsalted butter

Bring 4 cups of water plus 1 teaspoon salt to a boil in large heavy pot. Peel potatoes and cut them into ½-inch pieces. Cut the fronds off the fennel bulb and chop. Reserve. Trim any brown spots from fennel and cut bulb into ½-inch pieces. Put potatoes and fennel in boiling water.

Cook over medium heat for 40 minutes, or until very soft. Pass the potatoes and fennel through a potato ricer and return them to the pot to keep warm. Or transfer with a slotted spoon to a food processor and puree.

Add the butter and salt and freshly ground black pepper to taste. Mix in chopped fennel fronds.

Serves 6

Sugar Snaps in Orange Butter

A cross between garden peas and snow peas, sugar snap peas deliver what they promise: a sweet taste combined with a resonant crispness. Fresh orange juice adds perfume and emulsifies the butter into a delectable sauce.

1 pound sugar snap peas (see Note)

1 large orange

2 tablespoons unsalted butter, cold

Trim the ends of the snap peas and remove the strings running down the length of the pods.

Bring a medium-size pot of salted water to a boil. Add the sugar snaps and cook 3 minutes, or until tender but not too soft. Their color should remain a brilliant green.

Meanwhile, grate the orange zest on the medium-size holes of a box grater. Reserve. Cut the orange in half.

When the sugar snaps are done, drain well in a colander and put them back in the pot. Add the orange zest, juice of ½ orange, and the cold butter cut into small pieces. Heat slowly for 1 to 2 minutes until hot. Toss well. Add salt and pepper to taste. Serve warm.

Serves 4 to 6

ADD-ONS

Scatter 1 teaspoon of black sesame seeds on top for a striking color contrast.

Note: You can substitute snow peas.

Gratin Dauphinoise

A gratin is the golden, epicurean crust that forms on the surface of savory baked or broiled dishes. Pungent Gruyère cheese makes a genial topping that acts as a protective layer, preventing the potatoes from drying out.

The classic potato Dauphinoise (from the Dauphiné in France) is made with cream, but there's some debate about the cheese.

2½ pounds Yukon Gold or all-purpose
   potatoes

3 cups half-and-half

1½ cups shredded Gruyère cheese

Peel the potatoes with a vegetable peeler, making sure to remove any black spots. Slice potatoes paper-thin with a sharp knife and put them in a pot, along with the half-and-half, 2 teaspoons salt, and freshly ground white pepper. Stir well and simmer the potatoes in the half-and-half for 15 minutes, or until potatoes are just beginning to soften.

Preheat the oven to 350°.

Transfer the potatoes and half-and-half to a medium-size shallow casserole. The liquid should come just to the tops of the potatoes. Cover evenly with the shredded cheese.

Bake 35 to 40 minutes, until potatoes are tender and cheese is golden brown.

Serves 6 to 8

Dry-Curry Sweet Potatoes

My sister-in-law invented an intriguing preparation for this autumnal vegetable that we usually heap sweet things upon. Instead, she gives sweet potatoes a curry rub, which transforms them into savory, golden nuggets. Bet you can't eat just one.

1½ pounds medium-to-large sweet potatoes

2 tablespoons good-quality curry powder

2 tablespoons olive oil

Preheat the oven to 400°.

Peel the sweet potatoes, using a vegetable peeler, and cut them into 1-inch chunks. Place them in a medium-size, shallow casserole, sprinkle with the curry powder and 1 teaspoon salt, and then drizzle olive oil evenly over the top.

Bake the potatoes for 45 minutes, turning them once or twice so they brown evenly and don't stick. Serve immediately.

Serves 4

Barley-Buttermilk Salad

Barley is one of the oldest grains, going back to prehistoric times. Pearl barley—which has had the bran removed—absorbs flavors beautifully and is still extremely nutritious. Tossed with buttermilk dressing, it makes a tangy salad. Or serve it warm as an edible bed for Yogurt Chicken with Blackened Onions (page 145).

$\frac{3}{4}$ **cup uncooked pearl barley**

$\frac{1}{2}$ **cup buttermilk**

3 tablespoons chopped fresh cilantro

In a small enamel saucepan, bring 2¼ cups water and 1 teaspoon salt to a boil. Add the barley, lower the heat, and simmer 40 to 45 minutes, covered.

Drain well and put in a bowl. Add the buttermilk, the cilantro, and salt and pepper to taste. Mix well. Serve warm, at room temperature, or chilled. If barley becomes dry, add a little more buttermilk.

Makes 2½ cups, serving 4 to 5

Bay-Smoked Potatoes

Use extra-fragrant bay leaves and your house will be enveloped in Mediterranean warmth. Not only does this exceptional method of "smoking" add perfume, it also blesses the potatoes with a creamy interior. They look beautiful on a platter, glistening with oil under a garland of these dark-green leaves of the laurel family.

>**2 pounds small-to-medium all-purpose potatoes (about 8 to 10)**
>
>**14 California or Turkish bay leaves**
>
>**5 tablespoons extra-virgin olive oil**

Preheat the oven to 400°.

Wash and scrub the potatoes very thoroughly and dry completely. Toss with 3 tablespoons olive oil to coat.

Distribute the bay leaves evenly over the bottom of a heavy shallow casserole with a cover. Sprinkle with 1 tablespoon coarse salt. Place the potatoes on top and sprinkle them with 1 tablespoon coarse salt. Cover tightly, sealing with aluminum foil if necessary.

Bake for 1 hour. Remove from the oven. With a large spoon, transfer the potatoes and bay leaves to a platter. Cut the potatoes in half. Drizzle with remaining olive oil. Add additional coarse salt and freshly ground black pepper to taste.

Serves 4 to 5

Broccoli di Rape I-II-III

This leafy green vegetable with a slightly bitter taste is a favorite in our house. We look forward to its arrival and cook it in fanciful ways. Also known as broccolirab *in parts of southern Italy, it actually is the green leaves and stems of a large round turnip, correctly called* cime di rape.

I

1 pound broccoli di rape

1½ cups chicken broth

⅓ cup white raisins

II

1 pound broccoli di rape

¼ cup extra-virgin olive oil

4 small cloves garlic, sliced

III

1 pound broccoli di rape

Half of a 2-ounce can anchovy fillets in oil

2 tablespoons pignoli, lightly toasted (see Note)

I Trim the bottoms of the broccoli di rape. Wash well and pat dry with paper towels. Put in a heavy enamel pot with the broth and the raisins and cook over medium heat until tender, about 15 minutes. Remove broccoli di rape with tongs. Reduce broth, add salt and pepper to taste, and pour over top.

II Trim the bottoms of the broccoli di rape. Wash well and pat dry with paper towels. Put olive oil and garlic in a large heavy skillet and cook until garlic just begins to brown. Add broccoli di rape and a few tablespoons of water and cook until tender. Season with salt and pepper.

III Trim the bottoms of the broccoli di rape. Wash well and pat dry with paper towels. Chop the anchovies coarsely. Put the anchovies and all their oil in the bottom of a large nonstick skillet. Add the broccoli di rape and a few tablespoons of water. Cook over medium heat until tender. Season with pepper. Remove broccoli di rape and pan juices to platter. Top with toasted pignoli.

I, II, III: Serves 4

Note: To toast pignoli, put them in a small nonstick skillet and cook 30 seconds until they turn golden. Shake pan so pignoli do not stick or get scorched.

Chardonnay Cabbage

Slow braising in a budget-priced chardonnay gives this particularly friendless vegetable a fighting chance. Wine is a great coverup for cabbage's dreaded bouquet and mellows it into a side dish of softness and charm.

3 pounds green cabbage

3 cups California chardonnay

6 tablespoons unsalted butter, melted

Cut the cabbage into ¾-inch-thick slices. Soak in cold water mixed with 1 tablespoon coarse salt for 1 hour. Drain the cabbage and put it in a large, heavy saucepan. Barely cover with the wine. Cover pot and simmer over low heat for 1½ hours.

With a slotted spoon, remove the cabbage to a large bowl. Mix with melted butter. Quickly reduce the cooking liquid until syrupy and lightly browned. Pour over the cabbage. Add salt and freshly ground pepper.

Makes 8 cups, serving 8 to 10

ADD-ONS

Garnish with a chiffonade of fresh basil leaves, or for a different taste, 2 teaspoons caraway seeds.

Two-Way Grits

Grits, fashioned from coarsely ground hominy, either is or are America's answer to polenta. Stone-ground grits, white or yellow, give the best results.

I Cheddar-Pepper

1 cup quick-cooking grits

1 cup shredded sharp yellow Cheddar cheese

2 tablespoons unsalted butter

II Garlic

2 cloves garlic

1 cup quick-cooking grits

¼ cup extra-virgin olive oil

I Bring 4 cups water plus 1 teaspoon salt to a boil. Slowly add grits and stir well. Lower heat, cover, and cook 5 to 6 minutes, stirring twice. Remove cover and add cheese, butter, and lots of freshly ground black pepper. Stir until smooth.

If desired, pour grits into shallow casserole to 1-inch thickness and top with more shredded cheddar. Bake at 350° for 10 minutes.

II Bring 4 cups water, 1 teaspoon salt, and garlic cloves, pushed through garlic press, to a boil. Slowly add grits and stir well. Lower heat, cover, and cook 5 to 6 minutes, stirring twice. Remove cover and cook 1 to 2 minutes, until thick. Stir in the olive oil. Season to taste with salt and freshly ground white pepper.

I: *Unbaked—makes 4 cups, serving 6 to 8*
   Baked—serves 6 to 8
II: *Makes 3½ cups, serving 6 to 8*

Yucca "Hash Browns" with Red Pepper

ADD-ONS

Serve with hot sauce and a squeeze of lime.

If you've never been south of Palm Beach, quite probably you pass by yucca in your supermarket without ever making its acquaintance. Let me introduce you: It is one of those brown, tuberous things that you don't know what to do with but is wildly popular in Latin America and the Caribbean. This dish is so filling that you may as well forget a main course.

1¼ pounds yucca

¼ cup vegetable oil

1 large red pepper, seeded and finely chopped

Peel the yucca with a small, sharp knife and cut it into large chunks. Remove any woody parts. Place in a medium-size pot with salted water to cover. Bring to a boil, lower heat, cover, and cook for 20 to 30 minutes until soft. Drain.

Heat 3 tablespoons oil in a 10-inch nonstick skillet. Add yucca and chopped pepper and sauté 3 minutes. Mash with a wooden fork and cook over medium heat until golden. Turn over with a spatula. Add 1 tablespoon oil. With spatula, break up pancake into pieces to look like coarse hash brown potatoes. Continue to cook until crisp all over. Season with salt and freshly ground pepper to taste. Serve hot, cut into wedges.

Serves 4 to 6

Creamed Potatoes, Swedish-Style

I love the idea of pairing hot creamed potatoes with cold smoked salmon, which they regularly do in Sweden. They drink "snaps," a shot of ice-cold aquavit or vodka.

My friend Ulrika Bengtsson, chef to Sweden's consul general in New York, says to use Red Bliss or Yukon Gold potatoes for best results.

1½ pounds medium-size potatoes

2 tablespoons unsalted butter

1½ cups half-and-half

Peel the potatoes and dice into small cubes. Melt the butter in a large nonstick skillet and sauté potatoes for 2 minutes, being careful not to let them brown.

Pour the half-and-half over the potatoes and add 1½ teaspoons salt. Cover and cook 20 minutes, or until the potatoes are soft.

Serves 4 to 5 as a side dish, 8 as an accompaniment to smoked salmon or gravlax

ADD-ONS

Sprinkle potatoes with finely chopped dill. You can also add ½ cup chopped yellow onion when potatoes are sautéed, as is the custom in southern Sweden.

Wilted Cucumbers, Dill Butter

Most folks don't think about cooking their cucumbers. In fact, the pale-green flesh becomes unrecognizably tender, delicate, and as translucent as jade. This is a splendid use for a vegetable that otherwise has been relegated to the salad bowl.

4 large cucumbers

3 tablespoons unsalted butter

6 tablespoons freshly chopped dill

Peel cucumbers, cut in half lengthwise, and scoop out seeds. Cut the pieces in thirds, then lengthwise into ¼-inch-wide julienne.

Parboil in salted water for 5 minutes and drain. Keep warm in small pot, tightly covered.

Melt the butter in a skillet. Add the cucumbers and sauté 3 minutes. Toss with the dill and add salt and pepper to taste.

Serves 6 to 8

Wild Rice and Bulghur Toss

Elegant, earthy, and sweetly divine: A grass, a grain, and a grape. Serve with your holiday turkey, roast duck, or prime ribs. Or use as a nutritious base for a tasty grain salad. If you have any vegans coming to dinner, serve this with grilled portabello mushrooms for a classy repast.

½ cup wild rice, uncooked

1 cup coarse bulghur wheat

½ cup dried currants

Wash the rice and put it in a saucepan with 2 cups water and ½ teaspoon salt. Bring to a boil. Cover the pot, lower the heat, and simmer 45 to 55 minutes, until kernels are opened and tender but not mushy. Drain excess liquid.

Meanwhile, add bulghur to a pot with 2 cups water. Bring to a boil, cover pot, lower heat, and simmer 5 minutes. Turn off heat, add currants, cover, and let bulghur steam 10 minutes.

When rice is done, drain well in colander. Put in large bowl and mix gently with cooked bulghur. Add salt and freshly ground black pepper to taste. Toss with a fork to keep fluffy.

Serves 4 to 6

Braised Celery Batons,
Fried Celery Leaves

"Celery raw, develops the jaw.
But celery stewed, is more quietly chewed."

I've always loved this little ditty and invented this dish to honor Ogden Nash (although I refuse to eat my peas with honey).

1 bunch celery

2 medium cloves garlic

¼ cup olive oil

Remove the outer stalks from the celery, leaving the tender ones inside. Reserve the leaves. Save the outer stalks for another use.

Cut the inside stalks into 2-inch pieces and then into ¼-inch-thick julienne. You should have about 1 pound of celery batons.

Bring a large pot of salted water to a boil. Add the celery and boil 8 minutes. Drain in a colander under cold running water.

Cut the garlic into small pieces. Heat the oil in a medium-size pan and sauté the garlic until golden, about 2 minutes. Add celery and cook 10 minutes, or until tender. Remove from the pan with a slotted spoon. Add the celery leaves and fry 1 minute (adding a little more oil, if necessary). Serve immediately.

Serves 6

Baked Sweet Fennel, Parmesan Crust

Slow baking of these pale-green bulbs—sometimes called Florence fennel or sweet fennel—brings out their natural sugars, forming a sheen of caramel. Their anise-like flavor marries well with the sweet nutty taste of real Parmigiano-Reggiano.

3 medium-size fennel bulbs

3 tablespoons fruity olive oil

6 tablespoons grated Parmigiano-Reggiano

Preheat the oven to 400°.

Trim the fronds and stalks off the fennel bulbs and reserve for another use. Remove any dark spots from the fennel and trim the outside layer. Cut the fennel in half lengthwise through the root.

Place the bulbs cut side up in a shallow baking dish. Sprinkle with salt and freshly ground black pepper. Drizzle each piece with 1 teaspoon olive oil.

Bake 25 minutes. Turn the bulbs over, adding a little more oil if necessary. Lower the heat to 350° and bake 20 minutes longer.

Turn the fennel over so the cut side is up. Sprinkle each fennel half with 1 tablespoon grated Parmesan cheese and bake 5 minutes longer.

Serves 6

ADD-ONS

Sprinkle also with balsamic vinegar. For a trattoria-style main course, add sweet Italian sausage that has been crumbled and cooked.

Pan-Grilled Radicchio, Fried Rosemary

This pretty Italian white-veined magenta lettuce, related to chicory and endive, is at once bitter, peppery, and slightly acidic. Generally used in salads, it is excellent cooked, especially pan-grilled, when it gets a nice smoky overtone.

My garnish of edible fried rosemary was unexpectedly felicitous— even to me.

2 medium-large radicchio

¼ cup extra-virgin olive oil

8 sprigs of fresh rosemary, each about 2 inches long

Wash radicchio and remove any brown outer leaves. Cut radicchio in half lengthwise through the root end.

Heat a large nonstick skillet. Add the radicchio cut side down and press down with a spatula. The radicchio will blacken and get smoky. Turn over and repeat.

Turn again so that radicchio is cut side down. Add the oil, let it get hot, and immediately add the rosemary, which will get brown and crisp.

Remove the radicchio and rosemary to a platter and pour the oil over top. Sprinkle with coarse salt and serve hot.

Serves 4

French Potato Cake

Somewhere between a Jewish latke and Swiss rösti, these potatoes are first boiled, then grated and sautéed. The result is a thick and golden potato cake—crisp on the outside, creamy on the inside.

These potatoes "take the cake" when topped with Red Wine Apple Sauce (page 287) and sour cream, or crème fraîche and smoked fish. For a distinguished hors d'oeuvre, make them silver-dollar size and crown them with caviar.

> 1 pound Idaho potatoes
>
> 1 small yellow onion
>
> 3 tablespoons peanut oil

Wash the potatoes and put them in a pot with water to cover. Bring to a boil, lower the heat, and cook 15 to 20 minutes, until potatoes are just turning tender. Rinse under cold water. Peel and let cool completely.

Grate the potatoes on the large holes of a box grater. Put in a bowl. Peel the onion and grate on the large holes of the grater. You will have 1½ to 2 tablespoons onion "puree." Add the onions to the potatoes, along with ½ teaspoon salt and freshly ground black pepper.

In an 8-inch nonstick skillet, heat 1½ tablespoons of the oil. Pack in the potato mixture and cook over medium heat for 10 minutes, or until bottom is crisp. Slide the potato cake from the pan onto a plate. Place the pan upside down over the potato cake, then turn the plate and pan over so that the cake is now cooked side up. Add remaining oil and cook 10 minutes longer, or until both sides are browned and crisp.

Serves 4

Giant Glazed Onions, Balsamic Vinegar

Since 1978 I have been guest chef at the annual grape harvest of Clinton Vineyards in the beautiful Hudson Valley. These glorious onions were always part of the dinner buffet of local ingredients, where the Feders' award-winning sevyal blanc was featured.

3 very large yellow onions

4 tablespoons extra-virgin olive oil

3 tablespoons balsamic vinegar

Preheat the oven to 400°.

Peel the onions and cut them in half horizontally. Put cut side down in heavy shallow casserole. Pour 2 tablespoons of the oil over the onions. Add a sprinkling of coarse salt and freshly ground black pepper.

Bake 20 minutes. Cut side of onions will be black. Turn over and flatten with a spatula. Bake another 15 minutes. Turn again, flatten with a spatula, and bake another 20 minutes.

Remove the onions from the casserole. They should be soft and caramelized. Add the remaining 2 tablespoons oil and the vinegar to the pan. Pour the juices over the onions. Serve warm or at room temperature.

Serves 6

Crisp Eggplant Tassels

Also known as quaglie, *or* quails, *in Italian, small eggplants are cut so that they fan out like the bird's tail feathers. Certainly more romantic than "tassels," but then again they also look like "mops." No matter what you call them, they are lovely as a vegetable.*

4 baby Italian eggplants

Vegetable oil for frying

Balsamic vinegar or Herbes de Provence
   Vinegar (page 69)

Wash the eggplants. Make a series of parallel cuts, about ⅓ inch apart, starting 1 inch from the stem to the bottom of the eggplant, slicing completely through the eggplant. Be careful to begin 1 inch from the stem end so that eggplant remains intact. Roll the eggplants 90 degrees and cut again from stem to bottom.

Each eggplant will look like a tassel or mop.

Put the eggplants in salted water with a weight to keep them submerged. Soak for several hours. When ready to fry, remove from water and pat dry with paper towels.

Heat the oil in a large frying pan. The oil should be 1 to 1½ inches deep. Fry the eggplants on both sides until crisp and golden brown. Do not let them get too dark. Remove them from the oil with a slotted spoon and assemble them on a platter. Sprinkle with vinegar and dust lightly with salt.

Serves 4

Oven-Roasted Asparagus, Fried Capers

In less than ten minutes you can have the most addictive asparagus you've ever encountered. An intense dose of heat keeps these spears green and snappy. Deep-fried capers add a startling accent. A wonderful Mediterranean-inspired first course or side dish.

2 pounds medium-size asparagus

4 tablespoons olive oil

¼ cup large capers, drained

Preheat the oven to 500°.

Trim the stems of the asparagus, cutting off the ends. Drizzle 2 tablespoons of the olive oil on a baking sheet or jelly roll pan. Place the asparagus on the pan and coat with oil. Sprinkle lightly with salt. Roast for 8 minutes and transfer to warm platter.

Meanwhile, in a small skillet, heat the remaining 2 tablespoons oil. Fry the capers for 1 minute. Pour over the asparagus. Pass the pepper mill.

Serves 6

Saffron Orzo

Made in the style of its Northern Italian cousin, risotto alla Milanese, my orzo "giallo" also gets its luminescence from golden-orange saffron— a precious spice known for its singular flavor and exorbitant price. A little goes a very long way, and it will last a long time in your cupboard.

½ teaspoon chopped saffron threads

3 tablespoons unsalted butter

8 ounces orzo

Bring 2¾ cups water to a boil, let cool 5 minutes, and add saffron. Let sit 15 minutes.

In a medium-size heavy pot, melt the butter and stir in the orzo. Sauté a few minutes over medium heat, until orzo becomes golden.

Slowly add the saffron water and stir well with a wooden spoon. Add ½ teaspoon salt and freshly ground black pepper. Cover the pot and simmer for 10 minutes.

Uncover, increase the heat, and stir continuously for 5 minutes, or until all liquid is evaporated, resulting in a creamy-textured orzo.

Cover until ready to eat, then warm gently.

Makes 3 cups, serving 4 to 6

ADD-ONS

Add ¼ cup grated Parmesan cheese to orzo while hot. Stir well.

Cumin-Scented Couscous

Couscous, the pasta of North Africa and the Middle East, is processed semolina wheat formed into little seed-size "grains." Cumin seeds, when toasted, impart a musky flavor. Try the larger pearls of Israeli couscous (see Sources, page 289) for variety: both have great "mouth feel."

1¼ teaspoons cumin seeds

1½ cups homemade chicken broth (page 96)
   or canned

1 cup couscous

Toast the cumin seeds lightly in a nonstick skillet. Reserve.

In a medium saucepan, bring the chicken broth and cumin seeds to a boil. Lower the heat, add the couscous, and stir 2 or 3 minutes, until most of liquid is absorbed. Add salt and pepper. Cover. Keep warm until ready to serve.

Makes 4 cups, serving 6 to 8

ADD-ONS

Add ½ cup finely diced zucchini and a squeeze of fresh lemon to the chicken broth. Also nice with a pinch of cinnamon.

Aromatic Ginger Rice

Any long-grain rice will do for this elegant sidekick, but basmati is best. Originally from India but now grown in Texas and California, basmati rice has a lovely fragrance of its own. You'll want to keep some in your pantry.

3-inch piece fresh ginger

1 cup uncooked rice, long-grain white or
    basmati

2 tablespoons unsalted butter

Peel the ginger and mince half of it into very tiny cubes; you should have 1 tablespoon. Grate the remaining ginger on the large holes of a box grater. Place in a paper towel and squeeze into a small dish until you have 1 teaspoon ginger juice.

Bring 2 cups of water and 1 teaspoon coarse salt to a boil. Add the rice and the 1 tablespoon minced ginger. Cover, lower heat, and simmer 20 minutes, or until water is evaporated.

Melt the butter in a small pan and add the ginger juice. Drain the rice well. Add the melted ginger-butter and freshly ground white pepper.

Makes 3 cups, serving 6

ADD-ONS

Garnish rice with ¼ cup toasted pignoli (see note on page 197).

Egg Noodles with Butter and Rosemary

ADD-ONS

I like to add 1½ tablespoons of white wine when tossing the noodles with the butter.

Use broad noodles, or pappardelle, for making this noteworthy accompaniment to simple roasts. Or collect, as I do, bits of leftover dried pasta in a large jar—a pasta potpourri—for an added dimension.

1 pound broad egg noodles

6 tablespoons unsalted butter

1½ tablespoons fresh rosemary leaves

Bring salted water to a boil. Cook the egg noodles as directed on the package, being careful not to overcook.

Meanwhile, cut the butter into small pieces and reserve.

Snip the rosemary leaves so you have small irregular pieces, or mince with a very sharp knife.

When the noodles are cooked, drain well but do not rinse. Put in a warm bowl and toss with butter and rosemary, stirring carefully with a wooden spoon. Add salt and freshly ground black pepper to taste.

Serves 6

Orange and Gold Potato Puree, Sweet Potato Chips

Buttermilk adds old-fashioned richness to a dish that is simplicity itself and especially grand with its garnish of crisp sweet potato chips. You can also bake the sweet potatoes and fill the scooped-out shells with this autumnal puree.

> 2 pounds large sweet potatoes
>
> 1½ pounds Yukon Gold potatoes
>
> ⅔ cup buttermilk, at room temperature

Preheat the oven to 225°.

To make the sweet potato chips: Use ½ pound of the sweet potatoes (or half of a large sweet potato). Peel the sweet potato and slice into paper-thin rounds. Place the rounds on a large baking sheet. Bake 50 minutes, turning twice. They should become crisp and take on a bit of color. Do not let them brown. Sprinkle with salt and reserve.

To make the puree: Peel the remaining sweet potatoes and the potatoes. Cut them into large chunks and put them in a large pot with cold salted water to cover. Bring to a boil, lower heat, and cook 30 minutes, or until potatoes are very soft. Drain the water.

Mash the potatoes with a potato masher or put them through a ricer. Mix well, adding buttermilk until potatoes are creamy and smooth. Add salt and pepper to taste. Reheat gently before serving, adding 1 or 2 tablespoons buttermilk if needed. Stick sweet potato chips into puree.

Serves 6 to 8

Husk-Roasted Corn, Chili Butter

This unique method for cooking corn is especially good for a crowd. Blackening the husk imparts campfire flavor, while chili powder adds a smoky aroma. These look especially grand on a platter with the papery husks peeled back, giving you something to hold on to.

I wonder why they're called ears.

4 tablespoons (½ stick) unsalted butter

1 teaspoon good-quality chili powder

6 large ears of corn, in husks

Let the butter soften slightly. Mix well with chili powder and ¼ teaspoon salt. Roll into the shape of a small log, 1 inch in diameter (or put into a small ramekin). Refrigerate until firm.

Preheat the broiler. Sprinkle husks with water and place the corn on a baking sheet. Broil on all sides until husks turn black.

Lower the oven temperature to 500° and roast for 5 minutes. Peel back the husks with a clean kitchen towel, keeping the husk attached to the corn cob. Serve with thin slices of the chili butter.

Serves 6

Perfect Mashed Potatoes

Three ingredients never tasted so luxurious. These potatoes are so sinful, they're almost a sauce. Spending a few extra minutes pushing the potatoes through a sieve gives them ultra-smooth finesse. Fabulous topped with freshly steamed spinach kissed with lemon.

2 pounds russet potatoes

10 tablespoons (1¼ sticks) unsalted butter, cold

¾ cup light cream

Scrub the potatoes but do not peel them. Place in a pot with salted water to cover by 1 inch. Bring to a boil, lower heat, and simmer 30 minutes, or until tender. Drain immediately. Peel the potatoes when they are cool enough to handle.

Using a food mill or a potato masher, mash the potatoes well. Incorporate the butter bit by bit, stirring with a wooden spoon.

Heat the cream and slowly add it to potatoes. Season to taste with sea salt and freshly ground white pepper.

Pass the mixture through a large, fine sieve, using a large spoon, into a medium-size saucepan. Loosen with a few tablespoons cold water if necessary. Heat gently.

Serves 6 or more

ADD-ONS

Also delicious drizzled with vibrant Parsley Juice (page 218).

Parsley Juice

1 large bunch Italian parsley
2 tablespoons extra-virgin olive oil

Remove the leaves from the parsley. Blanch in boiling water for 1 minute. Plunge in cold water and drain. Puree in blender with ¼ cup cold water and oil. Process until smooth. Season to taste and strain through sieve.

Makes about 1½ cups

Tender White Beans with Tarragon

White beans are a wonderful foil for the singular taste of fresh tarragon.
In a gossamer dressing of fragrant, green oil and a little cooking liquid,
this salad/side dish satisfies—hot or cold.

> 1 pound Great Northern dried white beans
>
> 4½ tablespoons extra-virgin olive oil
>
> 2 tablespoons coarsely chopped fresh
>   tarragon leaves

Soak the beans in cold water for a minimum of 12 hours. Make sure beans are covered by 2 inches of water.

Drain the beans, rinse them well, and put in large heavy pot with water to cover. Add ½ teaspoon whole black peppercorns. Bring to a boil and let boil rapidly for 2 minutes, skimming any white foam from the top.

Lower the heat and simmer gently, uncovered, for 1¾ to 2 hours, until beans are tender but not mushy and falling apart. Add more water during cooking to keep the beans covered.

Drain the beans in a colander, saving ¼ cup of cooking liquid. Put the beans in a large bowl. Add olive oil and reserved cooking liquid.

Add coarse salt to taste, about 1½ teaspoons, and a pinch of white pepper. Add the tarragon and mix well. Serve hot or at room temperature, adding more olive oil, if desired.

Makes 5½ cups, serving 8 to 10

Ultra Tomatoes

Here are two methods for maximizing the flavor of tomatoes. The slow evaporation of moisture gives even pallid fruit a sweet, meaty taste. Slow-roasted tomatoes are not quite as dried as sun-dried—they have a distinctive texture and intensity of their own. This bright addition to salads and pastas makes monochromatic main courses come alive.

I *Slow-Roasted Romas*

12 roma (plum) tomatoes, halved lengthwise

3 tablespoons extra-virgin olive oil

3 cloves garlic, finely chopped

Preheat oven to 250°.

Place the tomatoes cut side up in a single layer on a baking sheet (you can line the pan with baking parchment).

Heat the oil in a small skillet. Add the chopped garlic and sauté 1 minute. Drizzle the oil and garlic over the tomatoes and sprinkle lightly with coarse salt.

Place the tomatoes in the oven and bake for 2½ to 3 hours. The tomatoes should retain their shape. Let cool.

ADD-ONS

Toss a handful of fresh thyme or rosemary over the tomatoes before baking.

II *Melted Tomatoes*

12 large ripe red tomatoes

3 tablespoons olive oil

6 large cloves garlic

Preheat the oven to 250°.

Bring a pot of water to a boil and boil the tomatoes for 1 minute. Drain and peel. Cut in half and seed. Put them on a foil-lined baking sheet, cut side down. Drizzle with oil. Sprinkle lightly with sea salt. Sprinkle a few cloves of crushed garlic over. Bake for 4 hours.

I, II: Makes 24 pieces

Chapter 11

Desserts and Other Sweet Things

*D*esserts are designed to tease. They are the ultimate temptation when one's appetite has largely been satisfied.

I'm not one who craves a sweet every day, but I simply swoon when the words "bonbon," "confection," or "confiture" come to mind.

Words like "candied" and "nectarous," "sugar-coated" and "honeyed," make me weak.

Images from long ago, like the brick of melting ice cream in Candy Land, transform me. Simple ideas like chocolate-covered cherries make me delirious.

Desserts are for when we go over the top.

Vanilla Sugar

4 cups granulated sugar
2 vanilla beans

Put the sugar in a large bowl. Split the vanilla beans in half lengthwise. With the tip of a knife, scrape out the vanilla seeds, reserving the pods, and add them to the sugar. Mix well with the fingertips, making sure the vanilla seeds are well distributed—they are moist and tend to stick together. Place the sugar in a large jar with the vanilla pods. Cover tightly and store in a cool, dark place.

Makes 4 cups

Cinnamon Sugar

2 cups granulated sugar
¼ cup good-quality ground cinnamon

Mix the sugar and cinnamon together in a bowl until thoroughly blended. Cover tightly and store in a cool, dark place.

Makes 4 cups

Green Apple and Lychee Tart

Fragrant and haunting, green apples and lychees make a compelling team atop crisp and buttery puff pastry pillows. The syrup from the lychees is reduced and used as a burnishing glaze. Serve with a cup of steamy green tea.

1 sheet frozen puff pastry, defrosted (about 8 ounces)

1 (12-ounce) can lychee nuts, in heavy syrup

2 Granny Smith apples

Preheat the oven to 375°.

Cut the puff pastry into 4 equal 5-inch squares. You may need to roll out dough slightly with a rolling pin. Keep it cold while you prepare the topping.

Drain the lychees well in a sieve, saving all the juice. Put the juice in a small heavy saucepan and reserve.

Cut the lychees in half and place them evenly on the pastry squares, leaving a ½-inch border. The lychees should completely cover the centers of the pastry squares.

Peel the apples. Core and seed them and slice them into very thin wedges. Arrange the slices in an overlapping pattern on top of the lychees. Arrange the squares on an ungreased baking sheet.

Bake for 15 to 20 minutes, until edges of pastry have puffed.

Meanwhile, reduce the syrup in the saucepan until it becomes a dark brown, thick glaze.

Glaze the tarts lightly with the reduced syrup, using a pastry brush, and bake 10 minutes longer. The pastry will be golden brown.

Remove the tarts from the oven. Brush with any remaining glaze.

ADD-ONS

Sprinkle 1 teaspoon Cinnamon Sugar (page 224) on top of each tart after initial glazing.

GRAPENOTE

Serve tart warm with a small glass of chilled Muscat de Beaumes-de-Venise or an Alsace late-harvest riesling.

Serve warm or at room temperature within 3 hours of baking. Serve with ice cream or whipped cream, if desired, especially if cutting in half to serve 8.

Makes 4 individual tarts, serving 4 or 8

Frozen Maple Soufflé

As if life weren't hectic enough, company's coming for dinner tonight! Here's an easy but elegant dessert you can serve with confidence. Its dulcet taste is worth every ounce of the costly maple syrup.

>   1 packet unflavored gelatin granules (1 scant
>   tablespoon)
>
>   2 cups maple syrup
>
>   2 cups heavy cream, whipped

Dissolve the gelatin in ½ cup cold water. Bring the maple syrup to a boil. Lower the heat and add the gelatin. Cook 2 minutes while stirring. Let stand until mixture begins to thicken. Slowly fold syrup into whipped cream, folding in well after each addition. Pour into parfait glasses and freeze.

Or you can put the mixture in a prepared 4-cup soufflé dish fitted with a foil collar, or in a nonstick 8-inch loaf pan, and freeze.

Serves 6

ADD-ONS

Garnish with crushed Almond Brittle from Sicily (page 269) or sprinkle with miniature semisweet chocolate chips. If serving from a loaf pan, slice thick and drizzle with Chocolate Maple Syrup (page 228).

Chocolate Maple Syrup

1 tablespoon pure maple syrup
2 tablespoons unsweetened cocoa powder
2 tablespoons unsalted butter

In a small saucepan, heat the syrup until hot. Remove the pan from the heat. Whisk in cocoa and butter until the mixture is smooth.

Makes ⅔ cup

Dark Chocolate Mousse

Mild obsession with a particular style of chocolate mousse is probably normal—and as personal and profound as the way one drinks coffee. I like my coffee black, my chocolate mousse intense.

ADD-ONS

Serve with rum-flavored whipped cream.

4 extra-large eggs, separated

7 ounces excellent-quality semisweet chocolate

⅓ cup hot, strong coffee

Separate the eggs. Chop the chocolate into small pieces. Place the chocolate, *hot* coffee, and egg yolks in a blender and blend thoroughly.

Beat the egg whites with a pinch of salt until stiff. Fold the egg whites together with the chocolate mixture. Mix gently but thoroughly.

Pour the mousse into a soufflé dish. Chill. Garnish with grated chocolate if desired.

Serves 6 to 8

Alice B. Toklas's
Sugar Candy

ADD-ONS

Scatter the top of the candy with finely chopped nuts before it cools.

I first encountered this recipe in the Alice B. Toklas Cookbook, *published in 1954. Alice, of course, was lover, confidante, and constant dining companion to the celebrated writer Gertrude Stein. According to Alice, "During the war there was a shortage of sugar, however this simple candy remained a staple of our household." Making this confection is like watching paint dry, but the results are well worth it.*

> 1 cup heavy cream
>
> 1 cup granulated sugar
>
> 1 teaspoon brandy

Put the ingredients in an enamel saucepan over low heat and stir constantly with a wooden spoon until the mixture is the color of coffee with cream. This will take 45 to 50 minutes.

Remove from the flame and pour onto an oiled marble slab or into a small nonstick square or rectangular pan so that the candy is ⅓-inch thick. Cool 20 minutes and cut into small squares.

Makes 24 to 32 pieces

Lemon Buttermilk Ice Cream

How luxurious only 2 grams of fat can taste!

2 cups superfine sugar

6 large lemons

1 quart buttermilk

Put the sugar in a medium-size bowl. Grate the zest of 2 or 3 lemons so that you have 2 tablespoons of zest. Juice as many lemons as needed to get ½ cup lemon juice. Add zest and juice to the sugar in the bowl and mix well.

Add the buttermilk and ⅛ teaspoon coarse salt and stir until sugar is dissolved. Chill 4 hours or overnight. Freeze in an ice-cream maker according to the manufacturer's instructions.

Serves 8

ADD-ONS

Serve on Strawberries in Grappa (page 232).

GRAPENOTES

Sensational with a glass of Asti Spumante.

Strawberries in Grappa

ADD-ONS

Garnish with sprigs of opal basil, lemon balm, or fresh mint. Delicious with Lemon Buttermilk Ice Cream (page 231) or a quenelle-shaped oval of mascarpone cheese.

The fire of grappa is softened here by the juice of sweet berries. Crowned with Lemon Buttermilk Ice Cream and a tuft of opal basil, this becomes a "sundae" for adults.

2 pints ripe fresh strawberries

1½ tablespoons sugar

¼ cup grappa

One hour before serving, wash the berries and remove the stems. Cut the large berries into quarters and the small berries in half. Place in a bowl. Toss with the sugar, the grappa, and a grinding of black pepper. Chill 1 hour.

Serves 4

Corsetière's Despair

Cunningly named by Lexie Dean Robertson from Rising Star, Texas, this peppermint-speckled frozen folly dates back to 1949—and looks it. It makes magic as it melts in your mouth and is as invigorating as a tumble in freshly fallen snow. A few drops of red food coloring slashed through the mixture with a knife produce swirls of brilliant red and soft hues of pink.

1 pound red-and-white-striped peppermint
    candy or candy canes

1 quart heavy cream

3 or 4 drops red food coloring

Coarsely chop one-third of the candy and reserve. Grind the remainder of the candy in a food processor until it is a fine powder.

Whip the cream with pinch of salt in large chilled bowl until stiff. Fold all the powdered candy and about half of the coarse pieces into the cream. Add the red food coloring, slashing through with knife to make red streaks.

Prepare a 2-quart soufflé dish with a foil collar: Fold a 3-foot length of aluminum foil in half lengthwise and wrap the soufflé dish with the foil; either tie the foil or hold it in place by folding its two ends together. Fill with the mixture and add remaining coarse candy on top. Freeze until hard, about 3 hours. Remove foil and serve. You also can make individual-size soufflés, which will freeze faster.

Serves 8 to 10

ADD-ONS

Serve with gobs of your favorite hot fudge sauce.

Pastel Easter Sorbet
(Kiwi and Galia Melon)

ADD-ONS

Drizzle each serving with 1 tablespoon crème de cassis or green chartreuse liqueur. Or you can add ½ tablespoon of each. For kids, top with a few colorful jellybeans.

Overexposed by the oddities of nouvelle cuisine, the kiwi is nonetheless an adorable fruit with good acidity and sweetness and decorative little seeds. Coupled with the intense perfume of a Galia melon from Israel, or the Cavaillon from France, it makes a simple water ice sublime. Substitute half of a ripe honeydew melon for the Galia, if you must.

> ¾ cup sugar
>
> 1 ripe Galia melon
>
> 3 kiwi

Place water in small saucer and ¼ cup of the sugar in another small saucer. Select six large white-wine glasses and dip their rims first in the water and then in the sugar. Repeat the process and place the glasses in the freezer.

Peel the Galia melon and the kiwi. Remove any seeds and membranes from the melon. Cut the fruit into 1-inch chunks and add to a food processor with pinch of salt. Puree until smooth. You should have 3 cups. Reserve.

In a small saucepan, boil the remaining ½ cup sugar and ½ cup water for 2 minutes. Let cool.

Mix fruit puree and sugar syrup. Chill several hours. Put in an ice-cream maker and proceed according to the manufacturer's instructions. Spoon into prepared wineglasses and freeze.

Serves 6

Chocolate Bread Pudding

It's rare to have leftover breakfast chocolate croissants, since they're hard to resist. But it's worth the restraint so you can make this newfangled bread pudding for lunch or dinner.

> **2 or 3 large day-old pain au chocolat**
>
> **1½ cups chocolate milk**
>
> **2 extra-large eggs**

Preheat the oven to 350°.

Slice the pain au chocolat into ½-inch slices. Let dry 30 minutes, then place in a 4-cup porcelain soufflé dish. The bread should fill the dish.

In a mixer, blend the milk, the eggs, and a pinch of salt until fluffy. Pour the mixture over the pain au chocolat, pressing the bread gently so that the milk covers the top. Let sit 5 minutes.

Bake 40 to 45 minutes. The bread pudding will look like a soufflé but will deflate as it cools. Serve slightly warm, or chilled if desired.

Serves 2

ADD-ONS

Add ½ cup of chocolate chips to mixture before baking. Serve with sweetened whipped cream dusted with cocoa powder. Delicious with a scoop of Bittersweet Cocoa Sorbet (page 248).

Iced Maple Custard, Warm Maple Syrup

This is crème caramel without the "caramel" (melted sugar) but rather with pure maple syrup acting as both a sweetener and a sauce. Its jolt of contrasts—cold, creamy custard anointed with warm, sticky sweet-ness—pleases the senses.

3 extra-large eggs, beaten

¾ cup pure maple syrup

2 cups half-and-half

Preheat the oven to 350°.

Combine the beaten eggs, ½ cup of the maple syrup, the half-and-half, and a pinch of salt. Pour the mixture into large glass custard cups.

Set the cups in a flat pan with sides as high as the cups and put the pan in the oven. Carefully pour very hot water to a depth of about half the cups' height. Bake 40 minutes, or until custards are just set. Let cool and refrigerate until very cold.

When ready to serve, gently warm the remaining ¼ cup maple syrup and serve drizzled on top. Or turn custards out of cups onto plates and drizzle syrup around the edges.

Serves 4

Black Walnut Bars

It was from my boss, the legendary restaurateur Joe Baum, that I learned about black walnuts. (Black walnut pound cake and Charlotte Russe are his favorite "desserts with nostalgia.") Here I combine these funky-smelling nuts in a confection something like a brownie. You will crave a glass of milk.

> 1½ cups honey-graham cracker crumbs
>
> 1½ cups coarsely chopped black walnuts (see Note)
>
> 1 (14-ounce) can sweetened condensed milk

Preheat the oven to 350°.

Put the graham cracker crumbs and walnuts in a medium-size bowl. Slowly add the condensed milk and a pinch of salt. Mix with a wooden spoon. Mixture will be very thick and gooey.

Pack into a nonstick 8-inch square pan, or into a 9½-inch round removable-bottom pan lined with baking parchment or coated with nonstick cooking spray. Wet your hands with cold water and smooth the dough on top.

Bake for 30 to 35 minutes. Let cool. Wrap the leftover cake very well in plastic wrap or aluminum foil. Keeps for weeks.

Serves 16

ADD-ONS

Add 1 teaspoon freshly grated orange zest. Also nice with a cup of chocolate chips or yogurt-covered raisins added to the batter.

GRAPENOTE

Have a small glass of oloroso sherry.

Note: You can substitute toasted regular walnuts for black walnuts. To toast, place on shallow pan in 350° oven for 5 minutes.

Chocolate Banana Terrine

This four-star recipe, inspired by Daniel Boulud, underscores the simple and sublime philosophy of Recipes 1-2-3: easy to make, great to look at, decadent to eat.

> 5 small to medium ripe bananas, peeled
>
> 1 cup heavy cream
>
> 1 pound excellent-quality bittersweet chocolate, chopped in small pieces

Line an 8- by 4-inch loaf pan with plastic wrap. Place the bananas in the pan to make 2 layers. In a small saucepan, bring the cream to a boil and melt the chocolate in the cream, stirring constantly with a wooden spoon. When the chocolate is completely melted and the mixture is smooth, pour it over the bananas. Let cool, then refrigerate overnight.

Unmold, remove plastic wrap, and serve in one ½-inch-thick slice or two thinner slices.

Optional: Puree one very ripe banana with a few tablespoons of water until very smooth. Serve alongside the terrine.

Serves 12

ADD-ONS

Serve with a dollop of vanilla ice cream and toasted slivered almonds.

GRAPENOTE

Nice with a glass of velvety Malmsey Madeira.

Prune Jelly with Prune Pips

From the cutting-edge 20th Century Cookbook, *published in 1897 in Rochester, New York, comes this mildly sinister recipe. Once you've mastered the arcane art of separating prune pips from their shells, it may become your "regular" dessert.*

> 1 pound prunes with pits
>
> ½ cup sugar
>
> 1 packet unflavored gelatin granules (1 scant tablespoon)

Pit the prunes and reserve the pits. Put the prunes, the sugar, and water to cover in a saucepan and cook over low heat for 2 hours. (Original recipe: While prunes are cooking, soak prune pits in boiling water for 30 minutes. Drain and reserve.)

Pass the prunes through a mesh sieve or a food mill, or puree until smooth in a food processor.

Soak the gelatin in 2 tablespoons cold water and add to prunes. (Original recipe: With the side of a big knife, break open the prune pits, remove the kernels, and add them to the prune jelly.)

Boil together for 2 minutes and pour into a 1-quart mold. Chill 2 hours, unmold, and serve.

Serves 6 to 8

ADD-ONS

You can substitute red wine for water when simmering the prunes. Serve with freshly whipped cream sweetened with confectioners' sugar and ¼ teaspooon almond extract.

GRAPENOTE

A small snifter of Armagnac gives this dessert a lot of class.

Fresh Blueberries, Lemon Curd Cream

ADD-ONS

Serve with Twice-Baked Oatcakes (page 32) for an amazing dessert combo.

The great food philosopher Curnonsky said, "Cuisine is when things taste like themselves." In season, then, this surely must be it!

1 cup heavy cream

½ cup lemon curd (see Note)

4 cups blueberries, picked over and washed

In a large chilled bowl, whip the cream by hand using a wire whisk. Whip until thick but still flowing (be careful not to overbeat). Fold in the lemon curd with a rubber spatula. Chill.

Serve over blueberries, saving some berries for a garnish.

Serves 6

Note: Lemon curd is available in some supermarkets and in specialty-food stores.

Chocolate Milk Pudding

Make this in the evening and eat it warm out of the pot. Save one portion for breakfast the next day.

⅓ cup cornstarch

Scant ½ cup good-quality cocoa powder

2½ cups Hershey's chocolate milk or Yoo-Hoo

In a heavy small-size saucepan, stir together the cornstarch and the cocoa powder. Slowly add the milk and stir in a pinch of salt. With a wooden spoon, stir slowly over medium heat, continually scraping the sides and bottom of the saucepan and breaking up lumps.

When mixture is smooth and beginning to thicken, stir more vigorously (you may decide to use a wire whisk at this point), lowering heat if necessary, and beat until very smooth and thick. Remove from heat and continue to stir 30 seconds. Pour into wineglasses or coffee cups.

Makes 2½ cups, serving 5

Chianti Granita

A granita is a coarse-textured sorbet, reminiscent of what Americans call "Italian ices." Traditionally made with coffee or fresh lemon juice, this version made with Chianti (or any other full-bodied Italian wine) is my gift to chefs everywhere. It is also a great way to use leftover wine!

ADD-ONS

Top granita with fresh raspberries and blueberries.

2 cups Chianti

6 tablespoons fresh orange juice

⅞ cup sugar

Put the Chianti, orange juice, and sugar and 2½ cups water in a heavy, nonreactive saucepan and simmer 2 to 3 minutes, until sugar is dissolved. Let cool.

Divide the mixture into two pie tins. Put in freezer. After 20 minutes, stir with a spoon, starting around the edges (this is where it freezes first). Repeat this process every 15 to 20 minutes (about 6 times) until mixture is frozen.

Scrape the surface of the frozen liquid with a spoon and put into chilled wineglasses.

Serves 6

Raspberry Cloud Soufflé

Soufflés scream "special occasion" to me, but this deceptively simple preparation is practical for everyday eating because it is remarkably low in fat! On fancy restaurant menus, soufflés are often expensive. This pink, sweet cloud is also cheap to make.

6 extra-large eggs

½ cup sugar

1½ cups excellent-quality raspberry jam, with seeds

Preheat the oven to 400°.

Separate the eggs, reserving 1 egg yolk and the 6 egg whites (save the remaining yolks for another use). Mix the egg yolk with 2 tablespoons of the sugar and brush the inside of a 6-cup soufflé dish with the egg yolk mixture. Set aside.

Melt the jam with 2 tablespoons water. Heat gently and keep warm.

Stiffly beat the egg whites with the remaining sugar until glossy. Using a rubber spatula, fold one-fourth of whites into the warm jam. Then add this mixture to the remaining whites, folding gently.

Prepare the soufflé dish with a 3-inch foil collar: Fold a 2-foot length of aluminum foil in half lengthwise; wrap the soufflé dish with the foil; either tie the foil or hold it in place by folding its two ends together. Spoon in the mixture and bake 15 to 18 minutes. Remove collar and serve immediately.

Serves 6

ADD-ONS

Add 1 to 2 tablespoons kirsch or crème de cassis to jam while warming.

GRAPENOTE

Serve with a kir royale (champagne and crème de cassis) or sweet Vouvray.

Green Melon Zabaglione

Andrew Wilkinson, once chef at the Rainbow Room, developed this twist on the traditional Italian version made with marsala. It has a pleasing chartreuse color, and its taste mystifies.

6 extra-large egg yolks

6 tablespoons sugar

6 tablespoons melon liqueur

In a double boiler, or in a bowl set over simmering water, beat the egg yolks and sugar with a wire whisk until they are light, fluffy, and lemon-colored. Continue to beat, slowly adding liqueur. Cook until thickened. The consistency should be like whipped cream.

Let custard cool a few minutes, whisk again, and pour into small wineglasses. Serve warm or chilled.

Serves 6

ADD-ONS

This custard is delicious served over a salad of chilled melon balls (honeydew, cantaloupe, Crenshaw) sprinkled with lime juice.

THE FOLLOWING PHOTOS DEPICT:

Dessserts and Other Sweet Things

1. Yogurt "Coeur à la Crème," Apricot Compote
2. Corsetière's Despair
3. Strawberry Flummery
4. Eggnog and Panettone Bread Pudding
5. Little Lemons Filled with Lemon Yogurt "Gelato";
   Pepper Lime Ice Cream; Amaretto "Creamsicle" in Frozen Oranges
6. Green Apple and Lychee Tart
7. Chocolate Banana Terrine
8. Turkish Cherry Bread

Maple Mousse Parfait

According to legend, Smith College girls in the early 1900s were fond of this. But it's a comforting dessert any generation will enjoy.

3 extra-large eggs, separated

½ cup pure maple syrup

1 cup heavy cream, whipped and chilled

Beat the yolks with an electric mixer until fluffy and lemon-colored, about 5 minutes. Add the maple syrup and cook in the top of a double boiler until the mixture becomes very thick, stirring often. Let cool completely.

Beat the egg whites with ⅛ teaspoon salt until stiff. Gently combine the cooled syrup mixture, egg whites, and whipped heavy cream until thoroughly incorporated.

Spoon into beautiful parfait or martini glasses. Chill.

Serves 6

ADD-ONS

Garnish with bittersweet chocolate shavings or candied violets.

Syrian Shortbread

Known as grabie *in its native Syria, this shortbread belongs in cookie jars everywhere. It is easier than traditional shortbread, just as buttery, and more tender.*

ADD-ONS

Delicious with a tall glass of Iced Bedouin Coffee (opposite).

> **1 cup (2 sticks) unsalted butter, at room temperature**
>
> **1 cup confectioners' sugar**
>
> **2 cups all-purpose flour**

Preheat the oven to 300°.

In the bowl of an electric mixer, cream the butter until light and fluffy. Add the sugar gradually, and cream thoroughly. Stir in the flour and add a pinch of salt. Continue to mix until a smooth ball of dough is formed.

Roll out the dough about ¼-inch thick on a board lightly coated with flour. Cut with a "doughnut-shaped" cutter 2½ inches in diameter, or use any decorative cookie cutter you desire. Bake on an ungreased baking sheet for about 25 minutes, or until the cookies are dry but pale in color. Remove from the baking sheet only when the cookies have cooled.

Makes 3 dozen

Iced Bedouin Coffee

Traditional Arabic coffee is served hot, black, and sweet. Usually prepared over an open fire in a special pot called a finjan, *it can also be made in large quantities in a medium-size saucepan, preferably one with a pouring spout. For hot summer days, I love this intensely flavored coffee served chilled over ice.*

> ¼ pound French roast coffee beans
> ½ tablespoon green cardamom pods
> Sugar to taste (optional)

Grind the coffee beans and cardamom together until very finely ground, almost powdery. Or buy Turkish coffee at a specialty coffee store or Middle Eastern food store. Bring 1 quart water to a boil. Add ½ cup ground coffee and stir quickly with the handle of a wooden spoon. Lower the heat and let the coffee come to a boil. As the foam starts to form and come to the top of the pot, yank the pot from the heat. Add sugar, if desired, and let cool. Strain coffee through a fine-mesh strainer and refrigerate until cold. Serve over ice.

Serves 6

Bittersweet Cocoa Sorbet

A sorbet with a winning texture. My friend, chef Chris Styler, says it tastes like a very elegant Tootsie Roll.

½ cup sugar (or Vanilla Sugar, see page 224)

½ cup good-quality cocoa

4 ounces unsweetened chocolate, chopped in
small pieces

In a medium-size saucepan, combine 1¾ cups water and the sugar. Bring to a boil. Whisk in the cocoa and chocolate.

When the mixture returns to a boil, remove from the heat and strain into a bowl. Let cool. Cover and refrigerate until very cold.

Process in an ice-cream maker according to the manufacturer's instructions.

Makes 2¼ cups, serving 4

ADD-ONS

Grate the zest of 1 orange into the mixture. Or add ¼ cup dark raisins soaked in whiskey.

Eggnog and Panettone Bread Pudding

A winter wonderland kind of dessert, since commercial eggnog usually appears just in time for the first frost.

8 ounces panettone

2 cups prepared eggnog plus 1 cup for sauce (see Note)

2 extra-large eggs

Preheat the oven to 350°.

Cut the panettone into ¾-inch cubes. Put them on a baking sheet and toast them lightly in the oven. Watch carefully. The panettone should become golden, not brown.

Beat the 2 cups eggnog and the eggs together using an electric mixer. Place the toasted panettone cubes in a baking dish that is 9×7 or 8 inches square. A glass dish is preferable. Pour the eggnog mixture over the panettone, pressing down so that the panettone is submerged. Let sit 15 minutes.

Place pan in a hot-water bath (bain-marie). Bake 40 minutes. Remove from oven and let cool. Serve at room temperature or cold.

To make the sauce: Put 1 cup eggnog in a small, heavy saucepan. Bring to a boil, reduce the heat, and simmer very slowly, stirring often, until the sauce is reduced to ½ cup and is dark tan in color. This will take 30 to 35 minutes. Let cool. Drizzle pudding with sauce.

Serves 6

Note: You can use a bottled eggnog, like Mr. Boston, from your liquor store. This will produce a deliciously "alcoholic" dessert. Or you can use eggnog that is available in the refrigerator case of your supermarket for a rich and evocative (but not alcoholic) pudding.

Oven-Roasted Strawberries, Fresh Strawberry Sorbet

In these days of oven-roasting everything for maximum flavor, chef Daniel Boulud has taken to putting giant berries in the oven. Great idea! He serves his with ice cream; I serve mine with sorbet. Either way, the very-berry essence of warm strawberries and icy frozen fruit provides a jovial blast.

ROASTED STRAWBERRIES

30 very large strawberries, stems removed

1 tablespoon unsalted butter, melted

3 tablespoons sugar

STRAWBERRY SORBET

2 pints ripe strawberries

½ cup superfine sugar

Juice of 1 lemon

To roast the strawberries: Preheat the oven to 400°. Place the strawberries, side by side, stem end down, in a baking dish. Add 1 tablespoon water to the dish. Brush the berries with the melted butter and sprinkle with sugar. Bake for 6 to 8 minutes, until the berries are soft. Serve warm with pan juices. Or serve with strawberry sorbet.

To make the sorbet: Remove the stems from the berries (you should have about 1 pound). Place in a food processor with 1 cup water, the sugar, and the lemon juice. Puree until smooth, strain, and freeze in an ice-cream maker according to the manufacturer's instructions.

Serves 6

ADD-ONS

Add seeds of 1 vanilla bean on top of strawberries before roasting. Garnish with lavender or mint.

GRAPENOTE

Splash Absolut Kurant over the sorbet.

"Love of Three Oranges"

I *Orange Ambrosia*

II *Marsala Oranges with Toasted Pignoli*

III *Orange, Walnut, and Pomegranate Salad*

Love of Three Oranges *is an opera by Prokofiev and has nothing to do with fruit, but I've always loved the image. My affection for these three orange recipes, however, is all about fruit and the combining of flavors with clarity and interest.*

I *Orange Ambrosia*

6 navel oranges

¼ cup Grand Marnier

½ cup unsweetened shredded coconut

Slice the ends off the oranges. Remove all the peel with a sharp knife. Slice the peeled oranges ¼ inch thick, remove the seeds, and arrange the orange slices on a platter. Sprinkle with Grand Marnier and chill 1 hour. Let the orange slices come to room temperature before serving. Sprinkle with the shredded coconut.

II *Marsala Oranges with Toasted Pignoli*

8 large oranges or blood oranges

6 tablespoons marsala wine

¼ cup pignoli, lightly toasted

Remove the skin from the oranges with a small sharp knife, leaving no white pith. Cut the oranges into segments, removing all the inner membranes. Put in a bowl and toss with the marsala.

Arrange the segments on dessert plates and sprinkle with the toasted pignoli.

ADD-ONS

Mix 3 tablespoons confectioners' sugar with 1 teaspoon ground cinnamon and sift over the walnuts. Or garnish the salad with ⅓ cup pomegranate seeds.

III *Orange, Walnut, and Pomegranate Salad*

This orange salad, which I use as a taste bridge between savory and sweet courses, is itself savory and sweet, with a coating of chopped walnuts and pomegranate molasses. It is also a refreshing dessert.

8 navel oranges, chilled

1 cup walnuts, toasted lightly and coarsely chopped

2 tablespoons pomegranate molasses (see Note)

With a serrated knife, cut away the orange peels and pith, discarding them, and cut the oranges crosswise into thin slices. Arrange the orange slices decoratively on a platter, overlapping slightly. The oranges can be prepared up to this point 4 hours ahead and chilled, covered with plastic wrap.

In a small bowl, stir the walnuts and pomegranate molasses together well. Cover the oranges with this mixture.

I: Serves 6
II and III: Serves 8

Note: Available at specialty-food shops and by mail order (page 290).

Cold Rhubarb Soup,
Mascarpone "Quenelle"

Sometime in the 1980s, fruit soups became popular desserts in upscale American restaurants. But they've been popular in many Eastern European countries for centuries. Refreshing, beautiful, and very springlike —and better for you than pie.

1¾ pounds rhubarb (about 1½ pounds trimmed)

¾ cup Vanilla Sugar (page 224)—or more (optional)

8 ounces mascarpone

Remove all the leaves from the rhubarb. Trim the stalks, wash them, and pat dry. Carefully cut the rhubarb into ¼-inch cubes. You should have approximately 5½ cups of diced rhubarb.

Bring 2 cups water and the sugar to a boil. Boil 1 minute, add rhubarb, and return to a boil. Lower the heat. Add a pinch of salt and a pinch of freshly ground black pepper. Simmer 10 minutes. Add 1 to 2 tablespoons additional vanilla sugar if you like it sweet. Simmer 1 minute longer. Let cool and refrigerate until very cold.

Ladle the soup into soup plates. Make quenelle shapes or egg shapes from mascarpone using 2 large tablespoons. Place one on top of each bowl of soup.

Serves 6

Vanilla Sugar "Cigars"

Since no one's smoking these days, why not serve sweet stogies that you can eat? Have fun rolling your own.

6 tablespoons unsalted butter, melted

12 sheets phyllo dough

¾ cup Vanilla Sugar or Cinnamon Sugar (page 224)

Preheat the oven to 350°.

Brush melted butter lightly over each of 12 phyllo sheets. Sprinkle each sheet with 2 teaspoons of the sugar.

Roll each sheet tightly to make a "cigar" that is 11 inches long and ½ inch wide. Brush with additional melted butter to cover the top of each cigar. Sprinkle each evenly with 1 teaspoon sugar.

Place on an ungreased baking sheet and bake 15 minutes, or until golden and crisp.

Makes 12 cigars

ADD-ONS

Add 2 tablespoons instant espresso to ¾ cup Vanilla Sugar and use the mixture to make Espresso Cigars. To ¾ cup Vanilla Sugar, add ¼ cup cocoa powder to make Chocolate Cigars.

Pepper Lime Ice Cream

First enigmatic, then addictive, these flavors tease and refresh the palate. Cool down, then meltdown. Particularly spectacular atop a puree of icy pink watermelon.

ADD-ONS

Splash with tequila. Serve in soup plates atop a puddle of chilled pureed watermelon or on a mound of diced mango.

2 cups superfine sugar

6 to 8 large limes

1 quart buttermilk

Put the sugar in a medium-size bowl. Grate enough of the lime rinds to make $1\frac{1}{2}$ tablespoons lime zest. Juice as many limes as needed to get $\frac{1}{2}$ cup lime juice. Add zest and juice to sugar in bowl and mix well.

Add the buttermilk, $\frac{1}{8}$ teaspoon kosher salt, and 1 tablespoon butcher-grind black pepper. Stir until the sugar is dissolved.

Chill 4 hours or overnight, then freeze in an ice-cream maker according to manufacturer's instructions. Serve in ice-cream dishes or in lime shells.

Makes $1\frac{1}{2}$ quarts, serving 8

Fresh Berry "Kir Imperial"

Nothing beats the simplicity and beauty of this drink-qua-dessert. Use tall champagne flutes and pile high with berries and bubbles. Use a good-quality demi-sec champagne or sparkling wine.

3 cups fresh ripe raspberries—plus more for garnish (optional)

1 bottle sparkling wine or champagne, chilled

1½ cups fresh blueberries—plus more for garnish (optional)

Put 8 champagne flutes in the freezer.

Put 1½ cups of the raspberries and 6 tablespoons of the champagne in a blender and puree until very smooth.

Remove the glasses from the freezer. In each glass, put 3 tablespoons raspberries and 3 tablespoons blueberries and pour some raspberry puree over the berries. Fill the glass to the top with champagne. Garnish with extra berries, if desired.

Serves 8

ADD-ONS

Garnish with fresh mint. Serve with Vanilla Sugar "Cigars" (page 255).

Little Lemons Filled with Lemon Yogurt "Gelato"

ADD-ONS

Garnish with sprigs of fresh lemon balm or lemon leaves.

This exhilarating yet simple dessert is dedicated to Trattoria da Paolino, also known as The Lemon Tree, in Capri, where one dines outdoors in a perfumed lemon grove . . . in a cool breeze.

> 10 large lemons: 6 whole lemons; grated zest of 2 lemons; ⅔ cup freshly squeezed lemon juice
>
> ⅞ cup superfine sugar
>
> 1½ cups plain yogurt

Combine the lemon juice, sugar, lemon zest, and ⅛ teaspoon coarse salt in a nonreactive bowl. Stir well until the sugar dissolves. Whisk in the yogurt and blend thoroughly. Chill overnight.

Cut a ⅓-inch "hat" off the tops of lemons, saving the tops. With a paring knife, cut out most of pulp from each lemon and then, with a spoon, scrape the remaining pulp from the sides. Turn the lemons upside down on paper towels to drain. If necessary, cut small slices off lemon bottoms so they can stand firmly.

Meanwhile, pour the yogurt mixture into an ice-cream maker and prepare according to the manufacturer's instructions.

Fill each lemon shell with ice cream, mounding it ½ inch over the top of the shell, and cover with the lemon "hat." Freeze until hard. Let sit at room temperature 10 to 15 minutes before serving.

Serves 6

Chocolate Truffle Torte

Pure gourmandise. This style of cake also has been known affectionately as "Chocolate Decadence," "Death by Chocolate," "Aunt Sonia's Chocolate Problem," and other such hedonistic names—all of which apply.

1½ pounds good-quality semisweet chocolate (Valrhona, if possible)

2 tablespoons unsalted butter

1½ cups heavy cream—plus ½ cup additional to be whipped for topping (optional)

Chop chocolate into small chunks and melt in the top of a double boiler over simmering water. Do not allow the chocolate to get too hot or it will seize up and become hard and dry. When the mixture is melted, remove it from the heat, put it in the bowl of an electric mixer, and whip with the butter and 1½ cups of the cream until all the ingredients are well incorporated.

Line the bottom of a 9-inch springform pan with waxed paper and pour the chocolate mixture into the pan. Let cool. Cover and chill for at least 8 hours.

Before serving, run the blade of a sharp knife around the edge of the cake to loosen it. Remove from the pan. Cut with a knife that has been dipped in hot water. If desired, whip the additional ½ cup heavy cream and serve with cake.

Serves 12 to 16

ADD-ONS

Add several table-spoons of grappa to the melted chocolate. Dust the cake with cocoa, or top it with fresh raspberries before chilling.

GRAPENOTE

An unexpected treat is a glass of lightly chilled Banyuls, a sweet red wine made from grenache; try one from Domaine de la Rectorie. Or serve a ruby port.

"Cannoli" Custard

Clemenza, in the movie The Godfather, *says, "Leave the gun. Take the cannolis." I say, keep the custard. Who needs the shells?*

2 cups part-skim ricotta cheese

9 tablespoons confectioners' sugar

¾ teaspoon rum extract

Gently whip the ricotta, sugar, and rum extract in the bowl of an electric mixer. Do not overblend. Divide equally among 3 or 4 martini glasses. Chill well. Sprinkle additional confectioners' sugar, through a coarse sieve, over the top of the custard just before serving.

Serves 4

ADD-ONS

Fold in ⅓ cup miniature chocolate chips or white raisins plumped in rum. Sprinkle crushed amaretti cookies or grated chocolate on top.

GRAPENOTES

Serve with ice-cold shots of Strega. Follow with a very short espresso.

Strawberry Summer Pudding

Invented by the English as an easy, peak-of-season berry dessert, my all-strawberry version relies on seasonally correct, ripe, red fruit bursting with juices and perfume. If you have the pleasure of picking your own from a local strawberry patch, select the ripest—even overripe berries—and rush home to make this dessert.

> 2 quarts very ripe strawberries
>
> 1¼ cups sugar
>
> 1 (1-pound) loaf good-quality sliced white bread

Reserve eight of the strawberries for a garnish and hull the remaining strawberries. Wash them in a colander and drain well. Transfer one-third of the hulled strawberries to a large flat-bottomed pot. Add the sugar and mash gently with a potato masher, leaving large pieces. Cut the remaining hulled berries in half. Add them to the pot, cook over high heat for 30 seconds, let cool, and reserve.

   Cut the crusts from the bread slices. Line the bottom and sides of 8-cup bowl with bread, cutting the bread so the bowl is covered completely, leaving no gaps. Spoon the berries and juices into the bread-lined bowl. Cover the top completely with more bread, again leaving no spaces. Select a plate that fits inside the bowl and place the plate on top of the bread. Put a weight on top of the plate, then wrap well with foil. Refrigerate for 8 to 12 hours.

   Just before serving, invert onto a large decorative platter. Spoon any juices over the top of the pudding. Garnish with the reserved whole berries.

Serves 8

ADD-ONS

Serve with whipped heavy cream, crème fraîche, or sour cream.

GRAPENOTE

How about a small shot of framboise?

Caramelized Pineapple, Black Pepper Syrup

Alchemy lesson: Start with an ordinary pineapple, poach it, and roast it, and you will have pineapple intensity of untold megabites. Add butcher-grind pepper for a little "black magic."

1 large ripe pineapple (about 3½ pounds)

1 cup sugar

1 pint good-quality vanilla ice cream

With a sharp knife, cut the skin off the pineapple, then cut the pineapple into six wedges. Remove the tough core.

Bring 4 cups water and ¾ cup of the sugar to a boil in a medium-size pot. Add the pineapple. Add enough water to cover the pineapple, if necessary. Lower the heat and cook 20 minutes, or until pineapple is tender but not too soft.

Remove the pineapple with tongs to a large squat glass jar or bowl. Reduce the syrup to 2 cups. Pour through a strainer over the pineapple. Let marinate overnight.

Remove the pineapple from the poaching liquid. Reduce the poaching liquid to 1 cup and add 1 teaspoon butcher-grind black pepper. Let cool.

Place the pineapple on a baking sheet and sprinkle heavily with the remaining ¼ cup granulated sugar. Broil until the pineapple begins to caramelize. Turn the pineapple and broil on each side for 1 minute.

Put the pineapple on dessert plates. Serve with vanilla ice cream and poaching liquid.

Serves 6

Poires Belle-Hélène, Pear Sorbet

Even the august chef Escoffier proclaimed, Faîtes simple: *something akin to "Keep it simple, stupid." Although he didn't actually subscribe to 1-2-3, he would have loved this simple preparation of his classic coupling of poached pears and chocolate sauce—named, no doubt, after the famous operetta by Offenbach.*

10 large pears, 6 with long stems

2 cups granulated sugar

¾ cup Chocolate Maple Syrup (page 228)

Carefully remove the skin from the 6 pears with long stems. Core from the bottom. Place the pears in a large heavy pot with water to cover. Add ½ cup sugar. Bring to a boil. Lower the heat, cover the pot, and poach the pears for 20 to 30 minutes, until just tender. Let cool in liquid. Chill until very cold. Reserve ½ cup cooking liquid.

Meanwhile, peel the remaining pears and cut into large chunks. Remove the core and any seeds. Put in a pot with 2 cups water and 1½ cups sugar. Cook until very soft; cooking time will vary depending on the pear. Puree in a food processor with the ½ cup reserved cooking liquid. Process until smooth. Chill several hours. Put mixture in ice-cream maker and make sorbet according to the manufacturer's instructions.

To serve, place a scoop of sorbet in a large goblet, top with a whole pear, and spoon chocolate sauce over the pear. Serve immediately.

Serves 6

ADD-ONS

Garnish with candied violets.

GRAPENOTES

Accompany with a glass of Poire William, straight from the freezer.

Pumpkin Pavé

Pavé means "slab," or "block," in French. This pavé tastes suspiciously like a Thanksgiving pie. It's very elegant when sliced and served with rosettes of whipped cream or drizzled with Chocolate Maple Syrup.

ADD-ONS

Put Chocolate Maple Syrup (page 228) in a squeeze bottle and drizzle over pavé.

5 extra-large eggs

4 cups (30 ounces) canned pumpkin pie filling

1 cup heavy cream

Preheat the oven to 350°.

In the bowl of an electric mixer, beat the eggs with pinch of salt until well blended. Add the pumpkin pie filling and mix until very smooth. Slowly add the heavy cream and continue to mix until smooth and creamy.

Pour the mixture into a nonstick 9½- by 5½-inch loaf pan. Bake in a hot water bath for 1½ hours.

Remove from the water bath and let cool, then refrigerate 3 or 4 hours.

Slice and place on chilled dessert plates. If desired, whip some additional heavy cream and serve the pavé with a dollop.

Serves 12

Yogurt "Coeur à la Crème," Apricot Compote

My inspiration came from a classic Turkish dessert of thickened yogurt sandwiched between poached apricot halves. But my results bear a striking resemblance to the classic coeur à la crème, *a rich cream-cheese dessert made in a heart-shaped mold. This ultra-rich-tasting dessert has no fat!*

> 1 pound large dried apricots
>
> 5 cups nonfat vanilla yogurt
>
> ¼ cup Tuaca liqueur (or any other orange-flavored liqueur)—plus more for drizzling if desired

Soak the apricots in 3 cups of water overnight.

Line a 7½-inch coarse mesh sieve with several layers of cheesecloth. Put the yogurt in the sieve and place over a bowl to catch drippings. Press down on the yogurt a few times to help release any liquid. Let drain 5 to 6 hours. The yogurt will become very dense and thick, turning into what is now called yogurt cheese.

Meanwhile, cook the apricots and soaking liquid in a covered pot over medium heat for 20 minutes. Mash lightly and add the ¼ cup liqueur. Cook 1 to 2 minutes, long enough to let most of the liquid evaporate but leaving the apricots juicy, not dry.

To serve, place all but 1 or 2 of the chilled apricots on a large round decorative tray or platter. Turn out yogurt cheese onto apricots. Slice the remaining apricots and use them to garnish the top. Cover with plastic wrap and chill until ready to serve. Sprinkle with additional liqueur if desired.

Serves 6

ADD-ONS

Garnish with chopped pistachio nuts or fresh mint.

GRAPENOTE

Remarkable with a glass of Hungarian Tokay with 4 to 6 "puttonyos," which signify the degrees of sweetness.

Napoleon of Roquefort and Sauternes

ADD-ONS

Before serving, dust the top with 1 tablespoon confectioners' sugar passed through a sieve or doily. You can add thinly sliced peeled pears to layers in napoleon or serve with grapes and walnuts. For a great little meal, accompany with Mesclun and Blood Orange Salad, Orange Vinaigrette (page 75).

GRAPENOTE

Serve a glass of costly-but-worth-it chilled Sauternes: Château d'Yquem or slightly more modest Château Climens.

A sophisticated dessert for those who don't love sweets. This delectable napoleon, layered with incomparable flavors of Roquefort and Sauternes, will leave you feeling richly rewarded, especially when it's served with a small glass of chilled Sauternes. Château d'Yquem, anyone?

1 sheet frozen puff pastry, defrosted (about 8 ounces)

5 or 6 ounces Roquefort cheese, at room temperature

¼ cup Sauternes

Preheat the oven to 375°.

Roll out the pastry to make a 9- by 9-inch square. Cut in half, put one piece on top of the other (you will have a rectangle), and press lightly. Bake 20 minutes, or until golden brown. Remove from oven.

Mix the cheese and the Sauternes in food processor until smooth. Cut the pastry horizontally into 3 equal layers. Spread half the cheese mixture on the bottom layer. Top with the second sheet of pastry and repeat. Cover with the third piece of pastry and press lightly. Refrigerate for several hours. When ready to serve, let napoleon come to room temperature.

Serves 8

Snitz Pie

A good apple pie goes a long way to assuring domestic tranquillity. No one will ever know that this pie begins with snitz—what the Pennsylvania Dutch call dried apples—but everyone will be happy.

3 cups dried apple slices

½ cup plus 1 tablespoon Vanilla Sugar (page 224)

Pastry for a 9-inch two-crust pie (see Note)

Soak apples overnight in 3 cups water. Cook in soaking water, covered, for 20 minutes, or until apples are very soft. Mash coarsely in a pot, using a wooden spoon. Cook 1 minute to let all water evaporate. Add the ½ cup vanilla sugar, mix well, and cook another minute. Let cool.

Preheat the oven to 425°.

Turn apple mixture into a pastry-lined pan, cover with the top crust, and crimp the crusts together. Make 2 or 3 slits to let the steam escape. Sprinkle with the 1 tablespoon remaining sugar.

Bake for 10 minutes. Reduce heat to 350° and bake 30 minutes longer. Let cool completely before serving.

Serves 8

ADD-ONS

Add ¼ teaspoon ground allspice to the mashed apples. Or serve with a small piece of sharp white cheddar cheese.

GRAPENOTE

How a about a snifter of Calvados to go with your coffee?

Note: You can use a good-quality frozen pie crust or make your own (page 268).

Flaky Pastry
for a 9-inch two-crust pie

2 cups flour
7 tablespoons unsalted butter, cold, cut into small pieces
2 teaspoons sugar

Place the flour, butter, and sugar and ½ teaspoon salt in a food processor and process until the mixture resembles coarse crumbs, about 10 seconds. Add 7 to 8 tablespoons ice water and pulse until the pastry begins to hold together.

Turn the pastry out onto waxed paper and flatten the dough into a circle. Add a little flour if dough is sticky. Wrap in waxed paper and refrigerate 1 hour.

Cut the dough into two pieces, making one piece a little larger than the other. The larger piece will be the bottom crust. At this point, you can freeze this dough for future use or proceed to make a pie.

On a lightly floured surface, roll out the larger piece and fit it into a 9-inch pie tin. Fill the pie. Roll out the smaller piece to a dimension large enough to cover the filling. Fold in half for easy handling and place atop pie. Unfold and fit the top crust onto the bottom crust. Crimp the edges together and you're ready for baking.

Almond Brittle from Sicily

With these basic ingredients, you can always make candy for company while filling your house with inviting aromas. This confection, known in Sicily as torrone di mandorle, *is truly authentic when made with almonds, but here in America you can use peanuts for a more patriotic brittle.*

1 pound sugar

1 pound shelled almonds or peanuts

½ lemon

In a large, heavy nonstick skillet or saucepan, heat the sugar and almonds over a very low flame, stirring constantly. The sugar will color slowly and crystallize around the almonds. This will take about 20 minutes.

The torrone is ready to be poured when the sugar is completely melted and a dark-brown color. Should sugar lumps form, be patient; they will dissolve if kept over a very low flame for 5 more minutes. Be careful not to let it burn.

Turn out onto a marble surface. Very carefully flatten into a thin sheet using the cut side of the lemon half. The mixture is very hot, so keep your fingers clear.

Let cool. Break into pieces using a hammer and a heavy knife.

Makes about 2 pounds

Mixed Fruit Rumtopf

ADD-ONS

Serve with English double cream or crème fraîche. Nice also with Sweet Zwieback (page 271).

Desserts for winter need to be lusty and comforting. Often we want something warm, or something showy enough to serve guests during the holiday season, so learn to flambé and add razzle-dazzle to this drunken fruit compote. The biscotti-like cookies are perfect for dunking.

1 pound mixed dried fruit

1 cup dark rum

½ cup sugar

Put the dried fruit, rum, and sugar in a large jar with a cover. Add water to cover—about 2½ to 3 cups. Cover and shake to help sugar dissolve.

Let sit for a minimum of three days in a cool, dark place, periodically adding water to barely cover. If storing longer, add rum from time to time to cover fruit. This gets even more delicious after one month.

When ready to serve, remove the fruit with a slotted spoon and cut into smaller pieces, if desired. Serve in goblets with liquid. Serve cold or warm. Flambé with rum if desired.

Serves 6 to 8

Sweet Zwieback

This simple little twice-baked cookie is somewhere between Jewish mandelbrot and Italian biscotti. Great for dunking, great for teething.

    2 eggs

    ⅔ cup Vanilla Sugar (page 224)

    1 cup flour

Preheat the oven to 400°.

Beat the eggs with a pinch of salt in an electric mixer for 5 to 6 minutes, until very thick and creamy. Add the vanilla sugar and beat 1 more minute. Lower speed and gradually add the flour.

Pour the batter into a nonstick 8-inch loaf pan. Bake 25 to 30 minutes (or until a toothpick comes out dry). Remove from the oven and let cool in the pan on a wire rack.

Lower the oven temperature to 275°.

Remove the loaf from the pan and slice into sixteen ¼-inch-thick slices. Put the slices on a baking sheet and bake 8 to 10 minutes on each side—until they just begin to color. Remove from the oven and let cool on a wire rack.

Makes 16 biscuits

ADD-ONS

Add 1 teaspoon anise seed to the batter.

GRAPENOTE

Wonderful for dunking into Vin Santo.

Spoonbread Pain Perdu

It's worth making a double portion of spoonbread custard to have enough for leftovers. This crisp and creamy preparation doubles as a dessert or a very tasty dish for brunch. Pain perdu means "lost bread" and has become synonymous with French toast.

½ recipe for Spoonbread Custard (page 188) (leftover is fine)

2 tablespoons unsalted butter

½ cup pure maple syrup

Cut the spoonbread custard into thick triangles. Melt the butter in a medium-size nonstick skillet with a cover. Sauté the spoonbread custard on each side for 1 or 2 minutes until crispy.

Cover the skillet and cook for 5 minutes over medium heat. The spoonbread custard will be hot and creamy on the inside, crisp on the outside. Serve with maple syrup.

Serves 3 to 4

ADD-ONS

This is lovely served with Strawberry Spoon Fruit (opposite) instead of maple syrup.

Strawberry Spoon Fruit

1 quart fully ripe fresh strawberries
1¼ cups sugar
1 tablespoon fresh lemon juice

Wash and hull the berries. Cut large berries in quarters and smaller ones in half.

In a medium-size enamel pot, alternate layers of berries and sugar. Bring to a boil, then cook over medium-high heat for 20 minutes.

With a slotted spoon, remove the fruit to a jar. Add lemon juice to the juices in the pot and boil over high heat for 10 minutes, until the juices are reduced by half and are thick and syrupy. Pour the syrup over the berries. Let cool, then refrigerate.

Makes 1 pint

Sliced Lemon Pie

This unlikely pie might inspire some controversy, since the lemons melt into a puckery, tart jelly. I enjoy its clean flavors immensely, especially with a cup of tea. You'll either love it or leave it.

4 medium-size lemons (about 12 ounces)

pastry for 9-inch two-crust pie (see Note)

1 cup Vanilla Sugar (page 224)

Preheat the oven to 300°.

Peel the lemons using a sharp knife, making sure white pith is completely removed. Slice lemons ⅛ inch thick. Remove any seeds.

Line a 9-inch pie tin with the pastry. Put the sugar in the pie shell in an even layer. Cover evenly with the lemon slices. Place the upper crust on top of the sliced lemons, pressing the edges very tightly to seal them.

Place the pie on a baking sheet and bake 1 hour.

Let cool completely before serving.

Serves 8 to 10

ADD-ONS

Scatter a dozen leaves of fresh tarragon on lemons before affixing top crust. Serve with unsweetened whipped cream.

Note: You can use a good-quality frozen pie crust or make your own (page 268).

Granola Fruit Cobbler

Ripe, juicy fruit is fundamental to this homey cobbler, also known as a crisp, crunch, or grunt. The more aromatic the fruit, the more luscious the results.

2 pounds very ripe stonefruit: nectarines, peaches, or plums

2 cups granola

5 tablespoons unsalted butter, at room temperature

Preheat the oven to 325°.

Peel the fruit and slice into ½-inch-thick wedges. Set aside.

Put 1 cup of the granola in the bowl of a food processor. Process until the granola is like coarse flour. Add 4 tablespoons of the butter and process until the mixture becomes a sticky ball.

Put the dough in a bowl and add the remaining cup of granola and a pinch of salt. Mix well with your hands until the mixture is crumbly.

Put the sliced fruit and 3 tablespoons water in a 6-cup soufflé dish or other ovenproof dish and dot with the remaining tablespoon of butter. Pack the granola mixture on top of the fruit to cover completely.

Bake 30 minutes. Serve warm but not right out of oven—let it sit at least 20 minutes. It's also good at room temperature.

Serves 6

ADD-ONS

Serve with butter-pecan ice cream.

Amaretto "Creamsicle" in Frozen Oranges

Frosty orange sherbet enrobing vanilla ice cream is a taste memory of my childhood—a time of innocence before anyone knew the word "sorbet." With an adult splash of amaretto, flavors intensify into a seductive new dessert.

1 quart mixed vanilla ice cream and orange sorbet

½ cup amaretto

8 navel oranges

Let the ice cream and sorbet soften slightly. Put in the bowl of an electric mixer or a food processor with ¼ cup of the amaretto. Mix until smooth. Work quickly so the ice cream doesn't get soupy. Place the mixture in the freezer.

Cut a ½-inch hat off the tops of 6 oranges. Scoop out the centers of the oranges, leaving 1 inch on the bottom. Fill the oranges high with the ice-cream mixture and place the hats on top. Refreeze.

Peel the remaining 2 oranges and cut them into segments between membranes, removing all the membrane. Put them in a bowl with the remaining ¼ cup amaretto. Serve as a garnish for the frozen oranges.

Serves 6

Grapefruit in Campari Syrup, Crystallized Grapefruit

Crystallizing grapefruit rind is a bit labor-intensive, and you don't need to do it; this refreshing dessert has its own charm. If you do make the effort to transform bitter citrus skin into delectable candy, however, the results will be spectacular.

> **5 very large grapefruits**
>
> **⅓ cup plus ¼ cup sugar**
>
> **2 tablespoons Campari**

Remove the rind of 2 grapefruits with a vegetable peeler and reserve.

Cut the skins completely off all the grapefruits, exposing the flesh. Remove all the white pith with a sharp knife. Cut between membranes to separate segments, removing all the membrane. Put in a bowl.

Collect all the juice and place it in a small pot with the ⅓ cup sugar, 1 cup water, and the Campari. Simmer for 15 minutes, or until the syrup is reduced to ¾ cup. Pour the syrup through a strainer over the grapefruit segments. Refrigerate until very cold.

Cut the pith from the reserved grapefruit rind and cut the rind into julienne strips ⅛ inch wide by 2 inches long. Place in a small saucepan, cover with water, and boil 20 minutes. Repeat the process two more times, discarding the cooking water each time. After cooking, put the rind and the ¼ cup sugar in the saucepan. Let simmer a few minutes until the sugar is incorporated and the skins are clear. Let cool.

To serve, place the grapefruit segments in overlapping circular fashion on dessert plates or in flat soup bowls. Pour several tablespoons of syrup over each and garnish with a mound of crystallized grapefruit.

Serves 6

Pots de Crème:
Chocolat et Vanille

Decidedly French, pots de crème refer simultaneously to little lidded cups and to the heavenly custard within. I like to serve two per guest— one vanilla, one chocolate—and to think about Paris in the twenties.

Au Chocolat

2 cups heavy cream

4 ounces good-quality semisweet chocolate, melted

3 egg yolks

Preheat the oven to 325°.

Heat the cream in a double boiler over simmering water. Add the chocolate and a pinch of salt and stir until mixture is blended.

Beat the egg yolks until light and lemon-colored and pour the hot cream over them, a little at a time, whisking constantly.

Pour the mixture into crème pots, small ramekins, or espresso cups. The shape and thickness of the container you use for baking will affect the timing. Cover with crème-pot covers or aluminum foil. Place the pots in a deep baking dish on the middle shelf. Pour enough hot water into the pan to come halfway up the side of the pots.

Bake until the center is set (barely jiggles when shaken), from 15 to 20 minutes. Remove from the water bath and let cool. Chill well.

À la Vanille

6 egg yolks

½ cup Vanilla Sugar (page 224)

2 cups light cream

Preheat the oven to 325°.

Beat the yolks until light and lemon-colored. Gradually beat in the vanilla sugar and a pinch of salt. Add ¼ cup of the cream.

Scald the remaining cream and gradually stir into the mixture. You will have about 3 cups.

Strain through a fine sieve into crème pots, small ramekins, or espresso cups. The shape and thickness of the container you use for baking will affect the timing. Cover with crème-pot covers or aluminum foil. Place the pots in a deep baking dish on the middle shelf. Pour enough hot water into the pan to come halfway up the side of the pots.

Bake until the center is set (barely jiggles when shaken), about 35 minutes. Remove from the water bath and let cool. Chill well.

Each flavor makes 6 servings

Chutney-Baked Apples, Vanilla Cream

ADD-ONS

Cover the tops of the apples with lightly toasted sliced almonds after baking.

An unexpected chutney filling brings out all the qualities you want in a baked apple: syrupy sweetness, good acidity, aromatic spices, an occasional raisin.

As for the cream, is there any way to improve on a pint of melted Häagen Dazs vanilla?

6 large Red Delicious or Rome apples

¾ cup mango chutney (Major Grey's)

1 pint super-premium vanilla ice cream

Preheat the oven to 400°.

Cut ¼ inch off the top of the apples. Core the apples, being careful not to cut through the bottom. Fill cavity with chutney and cover tops with a thin layer of chutney syrup.

Place in a baking pan with ½ inch of water. Bake 45 to 50 minutes, until the apples are soft but not falling apart.

Meanwhile, let the ice cream come to room temperature until it melts completely.

Remove the apples from the oven. Let them cool 15 to 20 minutes. Place in soup plates and pour vanilla "cream" around base of apples.

Serves 6

Frozen Hot Chocolate

I fondly recall this dessert, made famous at New York's Serendipity, where sophisticates celebrated their birthdays before they became sophisticated. The portion was huge, the chocolate slush numbed your mouth—what unforgettable fun! Keep a trayful in your freezer for "spontaneous consumption."

½ cup unsweetened Dutch-process cocoa

¾ cup sugar

2½ cups milk

Put the cocoa and sugar in a medium-size enamel saucepan. Add ½ cup of the milk to form a smooth paste. Slowly add the remaining milk and simmer until sugar dissolves and mixture is smooth. Let cool.

Pour the mixture into metal ice cube trays (it may stick to plastic) and freeze a minimum of 8 hours. Remove from trays and break up the frozen cubes with a fork.

Leave the food processor bowl fitted with a steel blade in the freezer for 1 hour. Then put in the broken-up cubes and 2 tablespoons water and process until smooth. Serve immediately in frozen coffee cups or goblets.

Serves 4 to 6

ADD-ONS

Serve with a dollop of sweetened whipped cream and a dusting of powdered cocoa. Tuck in a cinnamon stick or serve with warm Cinnamon Croûtes (page 282).

GRAPENOTE

Very adult with a soupçon of coffee-flavored liqueur, such as Tía María.

Cinnamon Croûtes

6 slices good-quality white bread
3 tablespoons apple butter
2 tablespoons Cinnamon Sugar (page 224)

Remove the crusts from the bread with sharp knife. Cut two 1½-inch round croûtes from each slice of bread with a cookie cutter. Brush one side completely with apple butter. Sprinkle with cinnamon sugar. Toast in oven until sugar melts.

Makes 12 croûtes

Hazelnut Tea Cake

Here's an easy way to have your cake and then eat it, for just when you think there's nothing to go with a cup of coffee, you can whip (literally) three simple ingredients into a lovely cake with a delicate crumb.

2 cups hazelnuts with skins (about 8 ounces)

2 extra-large eggs

½ cup pure maple syrup, plus 1 or 2 tablespoons for glaze

Preheat the oven to 350°.

Toast the nuts in a nonstick skillet until you just begin to smell a faint nutty odor. Let cool.

Put the eggs and syrup in a large warmed bowl. Add a pinch of salt and beat with an electric mixer at medium-high speed for 6 or 7 minutes, until the mixture has increased substantially in volume.

Grind the nuts finely in a food processor until powdery and mix into the egg mixture. Pour into a nonstick 8½-inch loaf pan lined with waxed paper on the bottom.

Bake 35 to 40 minutes, or until a toothpick inserted in the cake comes out clean. Glaze with 1 or 2 tablespoons maple syrup, spread with a pastry brush. Let cool.

Serves 8 to 10

ADD-ONS

Add grated zest of 1 orange to batter.

GRAPENOTE

Nice with sweet sherry such as Emilio Lustau's Pedro Ximinez Reserve, or orange-scented "Essencia" from Quady, in California

Turkish Cherry Bread

This unusual dessert is a sight to behold and lovely to eat. Fresh ruby cherries, gently poached, sit proudly atop a cinnamon-raisin sponge, soaking up glistening juices. Evanescent at best, the cherry season is short but sweet.

ADD-ONS

Add 2 tablespoons brandy to cherries while cooking.

1¼ pounds fresh ripe cherries

⅔ cup sugar

8 slices cinnamon-raisin bread

Pit the cherries, leaving as many whole as you can, or use a cherry pitter. If the cherries are ripe, it's easy to do this with your fingers.

Put the cherries in a nonreactive pot with the sugar. Let sit 30 minutes.

Meanwhile, put 2 slices of bread together and trim the crusts, making perfect squares. Repeat until you have 4 bread stacks. Toast the stacks well in the oven until browned and crisped on both sides. Place on a platter.

Add ⅓ cup water to the cherries and cook over medium-high heat for 15 minutes until soft. Pour the hot cherries and syrup evenly over the bread. Let cool.

Serves 4

Strawberries and Candied Ginger Dipped in Chocolate

Elemental flavors, basic and powerful. Have a bite of strawberry, then one of ginger, then strawberry. Continue until you have satisfied your craving.

> 6 ounces good-quality bittersweet or semisweet chocolate, chopped
>
> 16 large ripe strawberries with long stems
>
> 16 large pieces of crystallized ginger

In the top of a double boiler set over hot water, melt the chocolate, stirring occasionally. Remove the chocolate from the heat and keep it over hot water to keep it from becoming too thick.

Holding each strawberry by the stem, dip it into the chocolate, coating two-thirds of the berry. Let any excess drip off. Put the strawberries on a baking sheet lined with foil or waxed paper. Chill until hardened.

Pierce each piece of ginger with a toothpick and dip it into the chocolate to coat two-thirds, letting excess drip off. Place on a tray until hardened.

Makes 32 pieces

You can add 2 tablespoons unsalted butter or solid vegetable shortening to the melted chocolate for a shinier appearance. When the chocolate has set, you can "double-dip" strawberries and ginger in melted white chocolate, leaving a band of dark chocolate exposed.

Cranberry Chutney

Light brown sugar provides moderate sweetness against a backdrop of ultra-tart cranberries. It is, after all, the sweet-and-sour synergy that makes chutney chutney! Bits of candied ginger provide zings of intense flavor. This chutney ages well in your fridge.

4 cups cranberries

⅔ cup packed light brown sugar

2 tablespoons very finely minced candied
    ginger

Put the cranberries, sugar, and ginger and ⅔ cup water in a heavy, medium-size pot. Bring to a boil, lower the heat, add a pinch of salt and a pinch of freshly ground black pepper, and cook over medium heat for 8 to 10 minutes, until cranberries have popped and sauce has thickened. Chill well.

Makes about 2½ cups

Red Wine Apple Sauce

Often, a sweet grace note is desired alongside a holiday roast turkey, duck, or goose. On the Jewish holiday table, this apple sauce would cozy up smartly to a bold pot roast (page 168) and a crisp French Potato Cake (page 207).

6 large tart apples (about 2½ pounds)

2 tablespoons Cinnamon Sugar (page 224)

⅔ cup kosher sweet red wine

Peel and core the apples and cut them into large wedges. Put the apples, cinnamon sugar, and wine and some freshly ground black pepper in a medium-size nonreactive heavy pot with a cover. Bring to a boil, lower the heat, cover, and cook 15 minutes. Uncover and cook 10 minutes longer, or until most of the liquid has evaporated.

Mash lightly with a potato masher, leaving some chunks of apple. Chill well. This apple sauce can be made 4 to 5 days ahead.

Makes 3 cups

Sources

SPICES

*Local specialty-food stores and
Middle Eastern food stores*

ADRIANA'S CARAVAN
409 Vanderbilt Street
Brooklyn, NY 11218

800-316-0820

DEAN & DeLUCA
560 Broadway
New York, NY 10012

212-431-1691
800-221-7714

SULTAN'S DELIGHT
P.O. Box 090302
Brooklyn, NY 11209

800-852-5046

ISRAELI SPICES AND OLIVES

GREATER GALILEE GOURMET
2210 Wilshire Boulevard, Suite 829
Santa Monica, CA 90403

310-459-9120
Fax: 310-459-1276
800-290-1391

FLAVORED OILS AND VINEGARS

VINE VILLAGE
4059 Old Sonoma Road
Napa, CA 94559

707-255-4006

BALDUCCI'S
By mail order: 11-02 Queens Plaza South
Long Island City, NY 11101

800-BALDUCCI or 212-673-2600

WILLIAMS SONOMA
By mail order: P.O. Box 7456
San Francisco, CA 94120-7456

800-541-2233

CONSORZIO, NAPA VALLEY KITCHENS
910 Enterprise Way
Napa, CA 94558

707-967-1107
Fax: 707-967-1117
800-288-1089

POMEGRANATE MOLASSES, CHICKPEA FLOUR, HARISSA AND TAPENADE, BULGHUR, GRAPE LEAVES

Local Middle Eastern food stores

KALUSTYAN
123 Lexington Avenue
New York, NY 10016

212-685-3416

INTERNATIONAL TASTE
150 Seventh Avenue
Brooklyn, NY 11215

718-788-1999

SULTAN'S DELIGHT
P.O. Box 090302
Brooklyn, NY 11209

800-852-5046

DEAN & DELUCA
560 Broadway
New York, NY 10012

212-431-1691
800-221-7714

KING ARTHUR FLOUR (chickpea flour)
P.O. Box 876
Norwich, VT 05055

800-827-6836

OYSTER SAUCE, HOISIN SAUCE

Local supermarkets, specialty-food stores, and Asian markets

KAM MAN
200 Canal Street
New York, NY 10012

212-571-0330

WASABI POWDER AND PICKLED GINGER

Local specialty-food stores and Asian/Japanese markets

KATAGIRI
224 East 59th Street
New York, NY 10022

212-755-3566

SPECIALTY MUSTARDS AND CONDIMENTS

Specialty-food stores and supermarkets

MT. HOREB MUSTARD MUSEUM
109 East Main Street
Mount Horeb, WI 53572

608-437-3986
800-GET-MUST

GRACE'S MARKETPLACE
1237 Third Avenue
New York, NY 10021

212-737-0600

PURE MAPLE SYRUP

HIGHLAND SUGARWORKS
P.O. Box 486
Waitsfield, VT 05673

800-452-4012

SPECIALTY CHEESES

GALILEE CHEESE CORPORATION
(sheep's milk feta, labaneh)
P.O. Box 98
Tenafly, NJ 07670

201-569-3175
Fax: 201-569-3073

MOZZARELLA COMPANY
2944 Elm Street
Dallas, TX 75226

800-798-2954

BALDUCCI'S

800-BALDUCCI

TRUFFLE OIL, WILD MUSHROOMS, CAVIAR

URBANI USA
2924 40th Avenue
Long Island City, NY 11101

718-392-5050
Fax: 718-938-1704
800-5-URBANI

PASTRAMI-CURED SALMON

HOMARUS, INC.
76 Kisco Avenue
Mt. Kisco, NY 10549
Mail order: October 1 to April 1

800-666-8992

PERONA FARMS
350 Andover Sparta Road
Andover, NJ 07821

800-762-8569

BRESAOLA, PROSCIUTTO DI PARMA, SPECK

Local Italian specialty-food stores

BALDUCCI'S

800-BALDUCCI

PHYLLO DOUGH

THE FILLO FACTORY, INC.
56 Cortland Avenue
Dumont, NJ 07628

800-OK-FILLO

GARLIC SAUSAGES, FOIE GRAS, FREE-RANGE CHICKENS, DUCKS, ETC.

D'ARTAGNAN
399-419 St. Paul Avenue
Jersey City, NJ 07306

201-792-0748
Fax: 201-792-6113
800-327-8246

Cotechino, Zampone, and Italian Sausages

Local Italian specialty-food stores

Salumeria Biellese
378 Eighth Avenue
New York, NY 10001

212-736-7376

Specialty Sausages

Aidell's Sausage Co.
1625 Alvarado Street
San Leandro, CA 94577

510-614-5450
Fax: 510-614-2287
800-LINKS-95

Pancetta

Local Italian specialty-food stores

Zingerman's Delicatessen
422 Detroit Street
Ann Arbor, MI 48104

313-663-3400

Fresh and Smoked Meats, Poultry, Seafood, Caviar, Wild Berries, Dried Mushrooms

Polarica
73 Hudson Street
New York, NY 10013

800-426-3487

Fluted Candy Paper, Candied Violets

New York Cake & Baking Distributor
56 West 22nd Street
New York, NY 10010

212-675-2253
800-94-CAKE-9

Fat-Free, Low-Fat, Low-Calorie Recipes

FAT-FREE RECIPES

Port Consommé
Fennel, Leek, and Orzo Soup
"Fire and Ice" Gazpacho
Sauerkraut "Hangover" Soup
Curried Lentil Soup
Ginger Pepperpot, "Glass" Noodles
Pickled Greens
Cranberry Chutney
Herbes de Provence Vinegar
Labaneh (if made with nonfat yogurt)
Red Onion Salad
Red Wine Apple Sauce
Strawberries in Grappa
Pastel Easter Sorbet
Chianti Granita
Prune Jelly with Prune Pips
Mixed Fruit Rumtopf
Fresh Berry "Kir Imperial"
Grapefruit in Campari Syrup, Crystallized
    Grapefruit
Yogurt "Coeur à la Creme," Apricot Compote
    (if made with nonfat yogurt)
Iced Bedouin Coffee

LOW-FAT RECIPES

Party Food and Appetizers
5 grams of fat or less

Eggplant on Fire
Black Hummus
Tiny Pepper Cheese Crackers (1)
Med-Rim Lamb Nuggets
Angels and Archangels on Horseback
Fried Chickpeas with Sage and Walnut Oil
    ($1/4$-cup portion)
Rosettes of Smoked Salmon on Cucumber
    Rounds
Party Wraps: (1 wrap)
    Grape Leaves and Haloumi
    Radicchio and Smoked Mozzarella
Za'atar Pita (2 pieces)

First Courses
5 grams of fat or less

Celery Rémoulade, Celeriac Chips
Swedish Cured Salmon (3-ounce portion)

Soups
5 grams of fat or less

Yellow Turnip Soubise
Chilled Cauliflower Crème
Soupy Red Beans with Smoked Ham
An Unusual Borscht: Roasted Beet, Squash,
    and Yogurt
Yellow Pea and Bacon Potage

Main Courses
10 grams of fat or less

Tuna Burger, Hoisin, and Pickled Ginger
Pepper-Seared Tuna, Cool Mango Relish
Roast Pork Tenderloin with Prunes and Bay
    Leaves

Vegetables and Side Dishes
5 grams of fat or less

Zucchini, Black Olive, and Tomato
    Compote
Turkish Pilaf with Tomato
White Polenta with Parmigiano-Reggiano
Potato-Fennel Mash
Broccoli di Rape I
Cumin-Scented Couscous
Orange and Gold Potato Puree, Sweet
    Potato Chips
Barley-Buttermilk Salad
Wild Rice and Bulghur Toss
Aromatic Ginger Rice
Melted Tomatoes

Desserts
5 grams of fat or less

Orange Ambrosia
Little Lemons Filled with Lemon Yogurt
    "Gelato"
Turkish Cherry Bread
Strawberries and Candied Ginger Dipped in
    Chocolate (1 berry)
Lemon Buttermilk Ice Cream
Chocolate Milk Pudding
Kalouga (1 piece)
Oven-Roasted Strawberries, Fresh Strawber-
    ries Sorbet
Pepper Lime Ice Cream
Raspberry Cloud Soufflé

Miscellaneous
5 grams of fat or less

Beer Bread

LOW-CALORIE RECIPES

Party Food and Appetizers
Under 165 calories

Note: One ounce of potato chips has 150 calories.
Which would you rather have?

Cherry Tomato Bonbons
Black Hummus
Lemony Tahina
Eggplant on Fire
Za'atar Pita
Tiny Pepper Cheese Crackers (3)
Sherry Vinegar Mushrooms
Party Wraps:
    Grape Leaves and Haloumi (3 wraps)
    Radicchio and Smoked Mozzarella
        (2 wraps)

Fried Chickpeas with Sage and Walnut Oil
Rosettes of Smoked Salmon on Cucumber
    Rounds
Venetian Wafers
Med-Rim Lamb Nuggets
Angels and Archangels on Horseback
Ouzo Feta Spread (2 tablespoons)
Flying Saucers

First Courses
Under 165 Calories

Salmon Carpaccio Cooked on a Plate
Celery Rémoulade, Celeriac Chips
Grilled Shiitake Mushrooms, Garlic Essence
Salad Frisée with Lardons and Hot Vinegar
    Dressing
Arugula and Mussel Salad, Anchovy Vinai-
    grette
Salad of Roasted Beets and Beet Greens,
    Walnut Oil
Tomato, Mozzarella, and Basil: Six Styles (if
    mozzarella is 1 ounce or less)
Swedish Cured Salmon (3 ounces salmon)
Mesclun and Blood Orange Salad, Orange
    Vinaigrette

Soups
Under 165 Calories

Port Consommé
Fennel, Leek, and Orzo Soup
"Fire and Ice" Gazpacho
Yellow Turnip Soubise
Chilled Cauliflower Crème
Sauerkraut "Hangover" Soup
Soupy Red Beans with Smoked Ham
Curried Lentil Soup
An Unusual Borscht: Roasted Beet, Squash,
    and Yogurt
Yellow Pea and Bacon Potage
Ginger Pepper Pot, "Glass" Noodles

"Cream" of Spinach Soup
Avocado Velouté, Fino sherry
Chicken Broth 1-2-3
Fournade with Egyptian Spices
Carrot-Ginger Velvet
Red Wine Onion Soup

Main Courses
Under 350 Calories

Farfalle with Broccoli, Broccoli-Butter Sauce
Steamed Clams in Thyme Butter
Steamed Halibut, Bell Pepper Confetti
Rosemary-Infused Swordfish
Pan-Seared Tuna Niçoise, Tomato "Water"
Roast Pork Tenderloin with Prunes and Bay
    Leaves
Roast Cod with Red Pepper Puree
Salmon Baked in Grape Leaves
Tuna Burger, Hoisin, and Pickled Ginger
Pepper-Seared Tuna, Cool Mango Relish
Two-Way Salmon and Zucchini
Yogurt Chicken with Blackened Onions
Michael's Perfect Roast Turkey with Lemon
    and Sage (6-ounce portion)
Arista: Roast Pork Loin with Rosemary and
    Garlic
Braised Veal Roast with Leeks and Rosé Wine
    (6½-ounce portion)
Coffee and Vinegar Pot Roast (6-ounce
    portion)

Vegetables and Side Dishes
Under 165 Calories

Hubbard Squash and Orange Puree
Turkish Pilaf with Tomato
Steamed Broccoli, Stir-Fried Pecans
White Polenta with Parmigiano-Reggiano
Sugar Snaps in Orange Butter
Broccoli di Rape I-II-III
Wild Rice and Bulghur Toss

Caramelized Endive and Bacon
Spoonbread Custard
Braised Celery Batons, Fried Celery Leaves
French Potato Cake
Giant Glazed Onions, Balsamic Vinegar
Cumin-Scented Couscous
Zucchini, Black Olive, and Tomato Compote
Smothered Lettuce with Sumac
Potato-Fennel Mash
Barley-Buttermilk Salad
Wilted Cucumbers, Dill Butter
Watercress Puree
Yucca "Hash Browns" with Red Pepper
Pan-Grilled Radicchio, Fried Rosemary
Oven-Roasted Asparagus, Fried Capers

Desserts
Under 165 calories

Strawberries in Grappa
Pastel Easter Sorbet
Chianti Granita
Orange Ambrosia
Little Lemons Filled with Lemon Yogurt
    "Gelato"
Turkish Cherry Bread
Strawberries and Candied Ginger Dipped in
    Chocolate (2 berries)

Lemon Buttermilk Ice Cream
Prune Jelly with Prune Pips
Chocolate Milk Pudding
Kalouga (3 pieces)
Oven-Roasted Strawberries, Fresh Strawberry
    Sorbet
Pepper Lime Ice Cream
Mixed Fruit Rumtopf, Sweet Zwieback
Green Melon Zabaglione
Syrian Shortbread (1 piece)
Marsala Oranges with Toasted Pignoli
Vanilla-Sugar Cigars
Pumpkin Pavé

Miscellaneous

Beer Bread
Caraway Cheese Crisps
Twice-Baked Oatcakes
Iced Bedouin Coffee
Pickled Greens
Cranberry Chutney
Herbes de Provence Vinegar
Labaneh
Red Onion Salad
Melted Tomatoes
Red Wine Apple Sauce
Sweet Mustard Sauce

Index

beef (cont.)
prime ribs of, horseradish-rye crust, 173
steak haché, cabernet butter, 169
beer:
bread, 101
and Stilton soup, 100
beet(s):
and beet greens, salad of, walnut oil, 59
roasted, squash, and yogurt borscht, 103
beignets, little cod, 28
berry "kir imperial," fresh, 257
bittersweet cocoa sorbet, 248
blood orange and mesclun salad, orange vinaigrette, 75
blueberries, fresh, lemon curd cream, 240
blue cheese dressing, iceberg hearts, and bacon, 63
boccancini and pancetta, 43
borscht: roasted beet, squash, and yogurt, 103
bread pudding:
chocolate, 235
eggnog and panettone, 249
strawberry summer, 261
breads:
beer, 101
fried (flying saucers), 55
Turkish cherry, 284
bresaola and Asiago "carpaccio," truffle oil, 66
Brie and pear soup, 106
Brillat-Savarin's fondue, 54
brine-cured cornish hen, glazed shallots and parsnip puree, 147–48
broccoli:
farfalle with, broccoli-butter sauce, 116
steamed, stir-fried pecans, 187
broccoli di rape I-II-III, 196–97
broth, chicken, 1-2-3, 96
bulghur and wild rice toss, 203
butter(s):
-broccoli sauce, farfalle with broccoli, 116
cabernet, steak haché, 169
chili, husk-roasted corn, 216
dill, wilted cucumbers, 202
egg noodles with rosemary and, 214
orange, sugar snaps in, 191
pan-roast oysters with leeks and, 71
thyme, steamed clams in, 124
tomato, spinach fettuccine with, 121
buttermilk:
-barley salad, 194
lemon ice cream, 231

cabbage:
chardonnay, 198
Hungarian noodles and, 115
cabernet butter, steak haché, 169
calf's liver with home-dried grapes, 162
Camembert, la mort du, 31
Campari syrup, grapefruit in, crystallized grapefruit, 277
candied ginger and strawberries dipped in chocolate, 285
candy, Alice B. Toklas's sugar, 230
"cannoli" custard, 260
capers, fried, oven-roasted asparagus, 210
caramelized endive and bacon, 176
caramelized pineapple, black pepper syrup, 262
caraway cheese crisps, 104
carpaccio:
bresaola and Asiago, truffle oil, 66
salmon, cooked on a plate, 58
carrot(s):
diced, garlic sausage, lentils and, 161
-ginger velvet, 86
oven-roasting, 86n
cauliflower crème, chilled, 105
caviar, angel hair pasta with, 118
celery:
braised batons, fried celery leaves, 204
rémoulade, celeriac chips, 67
chardonnay cabbage, 198
checkerboard orzo salad, 72
Cheddar, farmhouse frittata, 62
Cheddar-pepper grits, 199
cheese:
Brillat-Savarin's fondue, 54
caraway crisps, 104
gratin Dauphinoise, 192
party wraps, 41–43
yogurt (labaneh), 111
see also specific types
cheese raviolini, roasted pumpkin sauce, 114
cherry bread, Turkish, 284
cherry tomato bonbons, 29
Chianti granita, 242
chicken:
broth 1-2-3, 96
country-fried, 142
in-a-watermelon, 143
lacquered wings, 44
perfect salad, 138
poulet rôti with wild mushrooms, 141

noodles:
egg, with butter and rosemary, 214
"glass," ginger pepperpot, 107
Hungarian cabbage and, 115

oatcakes, twice-baked, 32
oil:
basil, 156
burnt orange, red snapper in, 127
garlic, 52
and garlic spaghetti, 112
walnut, *see* walnut oil
olive(s):
black, osso buco with tomatoes and, 154
black, tapenade, 36
black, zucchini, and tomato compote, 183
green, sautéed duck breasts with sweet vermouth
and, 150
wine-baked, 51
onion(s):
blackened, yogurt chicken with, 145
giant glazed, balsamic vinegar, 208
red, salad, 132
red wine soup, 102
orange(s):
ambrosia, 251
blood, and mesclun salad, orange vinaigrette,
75
butter, sugar snaps in, 191
frozen, amaretto "creamsicle" in, 276
marsala, with toasted pignoli, 252
puree, Hubbard squash and, 179
red snapper in burnt oil of, 127
walnut, and pomegranate salad, 252–53
orange and gold potato puree, sweet potato chips,
215
orecchiette with endive and sun-dried tomatoes,
117
orzo:
checkerboard salad, 72
fennel, and leek soup, 93
saffron, 211
osso buco with tomatoes and black olives, 154
ouzo feta spread, 50
oysters:
angels on horseback, 46
pan-roast, with butter and leeks, 71
oyster sauce reduction, pan-seared sirloin, 170

pain perdu, spoonbread, 272

pancetta:
and boccancini, 43
crispy salmon with sage and, 128
panettone and eggnog bread pudding, 249
parfait, maple mousse, 245
Parmesan:
crust, baked sweet fennel, 205
lace galettes, 49
Parmigiano-Reggiano:
angel hair pasta with truffle oil, 119
white polenta with, 189
parsley juice, 218
parsnip puree, brine-cured cornish hens, glazed
shallots and, 147–48
party food and appetizers, 27–56
party wraps, 41–43
pasta, 110–22
angel hair, with caviar, 118
angel hair, with truffle oil, 119
checkerboard orzo salad, 72
cheese raviolini, roasted pumpkin sauce, 114
-cornmeal chips, 39
egg noodles with butter and rosemary, 214
farfalle with broccoli, broccoli-butter sauce,
116
fennel, leek, and orzo soup, 93
garlic and oil spaghetti, 112
ginger pepperpot, "glass" noodles, 107
Hungarian cabbage and noodles, 115
linguine Riviera, red sardine sauce, 113
macaroni and tomatoes, 120
orecchiette with endive and sun-dried tomatoes,
117
penne and pencil asparagus, torta di mascarpone,
122
saffron orzo, 211
spinach fettuccine with tomato butter, 121
veal tortellini, Turkish yogurt sauce, 110
pastry, pie, 268
pâté, extra-bonus mushroom, 38
pavé, pumpkin, 264
pea(s):
sugar snaps in orange butter, 191
sweet, puree, seared sea scallops on, 77–78
yellow, and bacon potage, 109
pear and Brie soup, 106
pear sorbet, poires belle-Hélène, 263
pecans, stir-fried, steamed broccoli, 187
penne and pencil asparagus, torta di mascarpone,
122